I'm Taking My Eggs and Going Home

How One Woman Dared to Say No to Motherhood

Lisa Manterfield

Advance Praise For

I'm Taking My Eggs and Going Home

" In this memoir of love and loss, Lisa Manterfield dares to reveal the depths of her desperation, and in so doing, dares to reveal the depths of her heart. "

~ Jennie Nash, author of
The Victoria's Secret Catalog Never Stops Coming
and Other Lessons I Learned From Breast Cancer

" *I'm Taking My Eggs And Going Home* is a wonderful book, full of heart and hope. As funny as it is moving. I couldn't put it down. "

~ Carrie Friedman, author of
Pregnant Pause: My Journey Through Obnoxious Questions,
Baby Lust, Meddling Relatives, and Pre-Partum Depression

" Lisa tackles a taboo subject with candor and aplomb. Her voice is a welcome sanity check for women left to wonder how society became so fixated on motherhood. "

~ Pamela Mahoney Tsigdinos, author of
Silent Sorority: A (Barren) Woman Gets Busy, Angry, Lost and Found

" A raw, transparent account of the gut-wrenching journey of infertility. Lisa writes with poetic, reckless abandon. Anyone who has ever suffered through infertility will thank her for pouring on the page the painful process of coming to terms with never being a mom. A true sister in the journey of infertility! "

~ Stephanie Baffone, LPCMH, NCC
Licensed and board certified mental health therapist and writer

I'm Taking My Eggs and Going Home

How One Woman Dared to Say No to Motherhood

Lisa Manterfield

Steel Rose Press

To protect the privacy of the persons involved, and in the interest
of narrative clarity, some names and details in this book
have been changed or altered.

Published by Steel Rose Press, Redondo Beach, California

Library of Congress Control Number: 2010913910

ISBN-10: 0-98301-250-4
ISBN-13: 978-0-9830125-0-4

Printed in the United States of America

Cover and book design by Julia Clarke
ScarletHare Design, www.scarlethare.com

For Jose
The One

I'm Taking My Eggs and Going Home

Prologue

I've made a decision: when my husband dies, I'm going to adopt a child. I'll wait until Jose's gone and then I'll become a mother by adopting through the foster care system. If I want to have children, I'm going to have to do it without him. It will be better for everyone this way, especially him. For five years we've tried to have a baby of our own. We've hopped from one crazy train to the next, from fertility doctors to Chinese Medicine Practitioners and around again; we've even dabbled in witchcraft. At my lowest point, I hatched a plot to steal another woman's baby. I cased the local hospital, found a glitch in security, and formulated my getaway plan. All I needed was a willing accomplice. But Jose's annoying practicality got in the way and my plan fell through. So now I'm on the crazy train all by myself, plotting a new scheme and wondering how much longer that same pesky husband is going to stick around.

It's a shame it has to be this way, but it's for his own good. We've witnessed what it takes to go through the foster/adopt process—mandatory visits with biological parents, the late-night arrival of a frightened child, the bitter disappointment when that child is taken away again. We understand what's involved in bringing a damaged child into our home. I'm prepared to do it, but I'm not prepared to put my husband through it. He's been through enough already, trying to fulfill my dreams. So, I'm just going to wait until he's dead. For his sake, I only hope it's quick and painless.

I glance across the living room, peeking at Jose over the top of the *Natural Health* magazine I'm pretending to read. The cat that has settled in my lap opens one eye and shifts into a new, even more comfortable position. Jose continues to tap away at his computer, surfing the Internet for a new bike he can't live without, oblivious to my plans for a future without him. I used to worry about the time he spent on his computer and cell phone; I was afraid of brain tumors and radiation-related cancers. I'm not afraid anymore; just curious if this is what will finally do him in. Or maybe he'll have a heart attack, a stroke, or the bike accident I've feared for so long. I'll take anything quick. I'm 39; I don't have time to nurse him through a long, drawn-out illness.

I'm surprised and somewhat perturbed to see that Jose looks pretty healthy. With all the stress I've put him through during the past five years, I'd expect him to look older, more haggard, just a little closer to death. It's so typical of him to be contrary and perk up just when I need him perking down. Under the instruction of all those damn fertility doctors, he's lost weight, lowered his cholesterol, brought his blood pressure back down into the safe zone. He's cut his wine consumption so low you'd think *he* was pregnant. This means that the fatty liver's probably not going to get him either. Maybe it will just be old age. Jose is fifteen years older than me, and once upon a time we wished it could have been different—that I'd been born earlier or he later, or that we'd met sooner. But when he was 20 and marrying for the first time, I was five and sneaking raspberry cookies from my best friend Simon, out of view of our teachers. Now the age difference should work to my advantage. The men on his mother's side barely make it past 50 and Jose has just turned 53, so the odds are in my favor.

I start to calculate how long I have if I still want to be eligible to adopt. I think I'm safe at 45; Jose's got six years to get busy dying in that case. But if he lasts more than *ten* years, I'll be 50. Will they still give a child to a 50-year-old single mom? And will I be able to handle it, especially with a child who will need special care? Would it be fair to raise a child with only one older parent? What if something happens to me? I need to get on with this.

It's a shame I have to do it without Jose, though. He would have been such a great dad. I can easily imagine him teaching our little girl to ride a bike or perching a little boy—a mini version of himself—in his lap and pressing his finger up to a flashlight so our son can see his bones inside. But Jose's no longer in the picture; he's not part of my plan. I don't know how much life he has left—maybe decades, maybe not—but I want the rest of our lives together to be good, even if it's short.

Lately, life hasn't been good at all and I wonder if he regrets marrying me. He's already done his family stint and has two grown children, but for five years—our entire married lives—we've been trying to have a baby together. He's been doing it for me—his young wife who always wanted a big family—and he's done whatever was required of him. He's had his testicles sliced open and stitched back together again; he's driven two hours L.A. traffic to be stuck with an acupuncturist's needles; he's been subjected to a steady regimen of pills and supplements, submitted to the hands of faith healers, masturbated into plastic cups, and provided me with sex-on-demand, whether he wanted it or not. He's held my hand while doctors performed miracle treatments on me and he's held all of me tight when I cried because they didn't work. So I'm not going to put him through it anymore. I'm just going to wait until he's dead and then I will become a mother.

He says he doesn't want a big funeral when he goes, but there are people who love him, who'll need to mourn his passing. I can picture the people who knew us when we were nothing more than friends. I can remember them saying how glad they were when we finally got together. They'll think I'm so brave when I maintain my composure. How will I tell them I've already made plans for my future? And how long should I wait before I put my plans into action?

For a second, I think about Jose being gone. I imagine his face without that smile I love so much. I see myself laying a single rose on his chest and kissing his cold, waxy cheek. I think about hearing *Summer Wind* again and knowing he's not there to dance with me. But I can't think about all this now; I have to think about my baby.

"I'm going to make tea," Jose suddenly says, getting up from his seat. "Would you like some?"

He catches me by surprise and intrudes on my dark fantasy. I check my facial expression and force it down into something more relaxed, stretching my eyebrows to iron out the thought wrinkle that always bunches between them, and letting my lips drop from their tight, pursed position into a neutral smile. He always knows when I'm deep in thought and will ask me what I'm thinking about. I hope he doesn't ask this time. I don't want to have to tell him, "I was making plans for when you're dead."

"I'd love some tea," I say in the most nonchalant voice I can muster. He has no idea of the scheme I've concocted. He's oblivious to the clock now ticking slowly down until his ultimate demise—a time bomb in an action movie, with me as the evil villain who's just pushed the big red button.

"Would you like a piece of gingerbread, too?" he asks, looking at me through sly eyes, as if he's asking me if I'd like to commit a cardinal sin with him. This is one of the things I most love about Jose—how he can make even the most innocent thing seem like a great adventure, how he takes the simplest of my British pleasures—tea and gingerbread—and gives it a passionate Latin twist. Whenever he asks me, "How would you like to come for a bike ride with me?" or "What do you say to a walk and a cup of coffee?" his eyes sparkle with the excitement of temptation and I know that if I go along, it's going to be the thrill of my life.

"Gingerbread?" I say. "Don't mind if I do."

He grins and disappears into the kitchen. In that moment, the dark balloon of my grim fantasy explodes and the absurdity of what I've been telling myself snaps in my face. My great plan, my infallible solution to all our problems is to wait for the man I love to die so that I can be a mother. This man who would walk over broken glass for me, the man I want to spend the rest of my life with, a man who can turn gingerbread into an erotic indulgence. I laugh out loud; it's the only decent response to my own twisted logic.

"What's that?" Jose calls from the kitchen.

"Nothing," I say, but it's not nothing; it's everything, and I very nearly threw it all away. I'm astounded that I might have allowed life with a wonderful man like my husband to pass me by while I just...waited. The idea that the precious moments we share every day, the simple things like a mutual love for gingerbread—the good, rich molasses kind—add up to nothing. The fact that I would fritter away the joy I have now for some unknown future, an imagined notion of personal fulfillment, some crazy elusive dream of the bliss of motherhood; it's nonsense. Waiting for Jose to die is the most deranged of all the deranged thoughts I've recently had. And this, right at this moment, is when I know this madness has to stop.

The past five years have changed us both. The two joyous people who stood barefoot beneath a gazebo in Napa and pledged to take care of one another forever are moving through life like two disconnected androids. The couple whose mutual passion bubbled beneath a surface of decorum for so long, until it could no longer be contained, now has sex once a month, if they're not too tired or in the middle of a fight, and only then for the sole purpose of attempted procreation. The adventuresome pair that traveled to exotic places, made impromptu trips to the opera, and planned great escapades together, now stay home, or worse, stay at work, to avoid the inevitable nightly conversation about children and doctors and fertile windows. And one of them is thinking that when the other dies, she can finally get what she wants. So it's time to make a drastic change.

I lift the sleeping cat from my lap, still in her curled position, and place her gently in the warm indentation I've just vacated on the couch. I step lightly to the kitchen door and watch my husband through the veil of a wooden bead curtain. He has warmed the teapot and the *his 'n' hers* mugs that my brother back in England gave us for Christmas. Mine says *Hippy Chick*; Jose's says *Big Fella*. (Jose wasn't sure if this was a dig at his waistline or a presumptuous statement about his manhood.) I watch as Jose slices two squares of gingerbread and places them on small blue-green plates—The Queen's Dishes, we call them—our one set of matching dinnerware that we usually bring out just for company. We haven't had a dinner party in more than two years and the dishes have slowly been relegated to daily use. Some are chipped or cracked; we've lost a couple to serious accidents; they're all a little the worse for wear.

The electric teakettle boils and clicks off and Jose drops a pyramid-shaped teabag into the teapot and tops it with boiling water. He stirs the pot, replaces the lid and covers it with the Union Jack tea cozy that my mother knitted for him and embroidered with his name. So many good memories in one short ritual. So many good times already stored away and so many more still to come. I can't just let our time together pass as if it's not important, as if all I'm doing is waiting for it to be over.

Jose senses me behind the curtain and turns my way. We've always had a kind of psychic connection; it's good to know that despite everything, it's still there. He smiles at me, his brown eyes twinkling. The smile is still there, too, and a little corner of my toughened, leathery heart softens again, reminding me that I wasn't always this crazy.

Not so long ago, I was just a woman who thought it would be wonderful to have children with a man like Jose, to raise them together and to form our sweet babies into intelligent, thoughtful adults. Children would have made life a great adventure. But standing there in the kitchen, I realize that life will have to be great without them, too.

1
The Siren Song of Motherhood
6 Years B.J. (Before Jose)

I was 28 years old when I found myself bouncing down
a mountain road in Ecuador, squashed into a seat built
for someone a foot shorter than me. My worldly
possessions were stashed in a backpack, slung on a rack
atop the bus, sandwiched between a bale of brightly
colored woven hammocks and a crate of live chickens.
I thought the guidebook was joking about the chickens.
The dusty windows were lowered in lieu of air
conditioning, but as the bus dropped down from the
chilly mountain town to the sweltering lowlands below,
the slight breeze became gradually less perceptible and
the cramped passengers began to sweat. It was a whole
afternoon's ride from Riobamba to Guayaquil and to pass
the time, the driver played a movie on a surprisingly
hi-tech screen. I watched as Cujo bared his teeth at his
victims and they exclaimed their horror in Spanish that
didn't match the movement of their mouths. Although
my boyfriend Mark and I were the only *gringos* on the
bus (travelers, not tourists), most of the other passengers
were Quichua-speaking Indians, so I wasn't the only
one who didn't understand the dialogue. As Cujo tore

another victim to smithereens, I realized that the words weren't important anyway. Still, it seemed an inappropriate movie for a public bus, and I looked around to see if there were children watching. Across the aisle, a wide-eyed little boy stared in fascination—not at the horror movie, but at me. His dirty cheeks pouched out around orange soda colored lips and his dark, almost black eyes were fixed firmly on my pale *gringa* face. He was beautiful—a tough, scrappy little boy, with all the innocence of his three years. And that's when I heard it—the siren song of Motherhood.

I wanted to reach across and pull the little boy into my lap. I wanted to hold him close to me and brush the tangled hair away from his eyes. I wanted to sing songs and tell him silly stories until he laughed that uncontrollable little boy laugh. He'd laugh so hard, he'd wear himself out and finally fall asleep in my arms. I could feel the desire tugging at me, harder than I'd ever felt it before, and I knew without a doubt that I wanted to be a mother. I was 28 years old, already once-divorced, and all I had to show for it were a cubic zirconium ring, a name I wasn't born with, and the backside of my first decade of adulthood. I had a lot of lost time to recover.

I looked over at Mark sleeping in the seat beside me, and wondered if he was The One. We'd been together for a year and we were a compatible couple; we thought alike, shared a passion for travel, and I liked the way he behaved around kids. He had a spirit of adventure and a *joie de vivre* that drew children towards him. I thought he'd be a fun dad.

The next decade of my life was coming at me and I needed to think about my long-term plans. I couldn't keep riding rickety buses with nothing but a backpack and a stash of Ecuadorian Sucre in my socks, and surely Mark couldn't either. He was heading for 40, but insisted he didn't want kids. He was a free spirit and loved his lifestyle; if he had children that would all end. We *did* have a good life. We worked long, erratic film industry hours, saved our money, and then we traveled. We couldn't do that with a young family, but we couldn't be nomads forever either. Could we?

Mark woke up and the little boy switched his attention. He stared wide-eyed as Mark played peek-a-boo behind his hands, popping out with a surprised clown look on his face. The little boy laughed, his mother smiled, and Mark offered them both some *melcochas,* sweet Ecuadorian toffee. Watching him in action, I decided I'd stick around. He was a good man and a natural with kids. Sooner or later, he was bound to change his mind.

Bound to change his mind. I wasn't an idiot; I knew how that sounded. I'd learned a thing or two about men and one thing I knew for sure was that you couldn't change them. No matter how charming you were or how intelligently you argued your case, you couldn't change a conservative into a liberal, a homebody into an adventurer, or a sports nut into a theater-lover. Been there, tried that, hence one ex-husband. The old adage that a woman marries a man hoping he'll change and a man marries a woman hoping she won't, would be funny if it wasn't so true. But the whole kid thing was different. I could understand Mark wanting to live the free-spirited, single life, but sooner or later, a man had to think of his future. He had to consider his advancing years and the prospect of being alone. And no one really wanted to be alone. Did they? Everybody needed somebody, surely, and eventually that somebody would want a little somebody to make the family complete. Sooner or later his male equivalent of a biological clock would have to kick in. I knew he'd been looking for the right woman to settle down with—he'd told me as much—and I was pretty sure that he'd found her in me. So, I knew we'd have kids together eventually and I was willing to wait; we still had plenty of time.

Two years later and we'd just returned from a Northern California visit with Mark's family. He'd been gone for two weeks, but my schedule had permitted only a long weekend. He was sifting through the stack of mail and I was sorting dirty laundry, menial work for a big conversation.

"My mom says you're nesting," he said, out of the blue.

"Really?" I said, looking around at the grubby cream walls and the standard Rental Beige carpet in our dim apartment. There was no evidence here of anybody nesting. Yes, I'd made plans to paint the living room, hoping the contrast between clean and not would prompt Mark into agreeing to new curtains, some decent lighting and maybe even a nice couch. The place could have used some plants and a wall of framed photographs of our families and our various trips. If I had my way, the hideous, dust-collecting mushroom lamps he insisted on keeping on full display would be relegated to the back room, a closet, or preferably The Salvation Army. The whole place needed sprucing up, but the rent hadn't been raised in years so we didn't rile the landlord. This was a temporary residence for us, as far as I was concerned, and I was ready to move from the dingy old apartment with its cottage cheese ceilings and thin walls, to somewhere with a backyard full of flowers and a vegetable patch, a house cat, and more than likely, children. If I was going to build a nest, it wouldn't be in this tree.

But I had to admit that, since my 30th birthday, my priorities had changed. I'd settled into a stable corporate job and traded vacation time for health insurance and a 401K. I was starting to think about putting down roots, making a home, and filling it with a family. One by one, our friends were getting married, buying houses and having children. They were where I wanted to be and I was nowhere close. So, while Mark was itching to go backpacking in Southeast Asia, I was hoarding Personal Time Off to spend time with my family in England. While he was working crazy hours and raking in the overtime, saving for the next big trip, I was picking out paint colors and trying to turn a north-facing balcony into a garden. He was making out-of-town trips without me, and I had bought a goldfish—a semi-permanent pet—for something to nurture.

"My mom says I need to watch out because you're getting broody," he said.

"What?" I said, puffing up with righteous indignation and choking back a sly smile at his mother's hawk-like observations, knowing how pleased she would be if I was. We'd spent most of my portion of the Northern California trip with Mark's sister and her family, with as much time as possible spent with their two young girls. The four of us had gone to the nearby park, walking hand-in-hand like a necklace of alternating-sized beads. We'd stopped for pizza on the way home, and when the sun went down, Katie, the six-year-old had put on pajamas and handed me the *Paddington Bear* book I'd given her the previous Christmas. It had been my favorite book as a child, given to me on my eighth birthday by my older brother, Ben. It had been a treasured gift and was one of the books I most enjoyed sharing with children.

I had taken the book from Katie and helped her climb into my lap. It was just the two of us; the others were in another room watching TV. She settled down into my lap and pressed her thin warm body against me.

The smell of watermelon shampoo drifted up from her damp hair and her pajamas still carried the faint aroma of sleeping little girl from the previous night. I squashed her closer and cracked open the book.

"Mr. and Mrs. Brown first met Paddington on a railway platform," I began in my best storytelling voice. I felt her body relax into mine as the story of the little bear from darkest Peru, a place I had been, unfolded.

I read aloud, doing appropriate voices for each of the Brown family members and a little-bear-lost voice for Paddington himself. I kept reading long after Katie had fallen asleep, until finally I put the book down and carried her upstairs to bed. I tucked the blankets around her and whispered, "Goodnight."

If this was what Mark's mother had interpreted as broody, she was right. I did want a little girl of my own; I was tired of tucking other people's children into bed. What had once been an assumption of something that would happen someday had now become a burning desire. I was ready to be a mother and I wanted Mark to be ready, too.

I looked over at Mark. He was poring over a credit card statement, crosschecking every item for accuracy. His attention to detail was a good trait, I thought; it made up for my own fly-by-the-seat-of-my-pants way of doing things. He'd be a responsible father, a hands-on type, who'd want a say in nutrition and education, and would have opinions on how to best raise a child. Those opinions would hopefully mesh with mine. But he seemed to have a deep-rooted fear of that level of commitment, or any commitment at all.

Technically, we were engaged, insofar as I had a ring that we'd bought, after much discussion of its significance, during a cruise to the Virgin Islands. Actually, the ring I was wearing wasn't the one we'd originally bought. He'd sent that one back once we were home and had a local jeweler, who he deemed more trustworthy, replicate the ring with better quality stones. I liked the original better, even if the diamond was flawed.

We almost got married on the cruise ship, the night we'd bought the ring. Out on deck, we'd cracked open a bottle of champagne to celebrate our engagement and as the bubbles of alcohol hit our bloodstream and the cool Caribbean breeze whipped off the bow of the ship and through our hair, we'd curled up on a sun lounger and discussed the idea of being married by the ship's captain. It was such a romantic notion, an impromptu wedding at sea, a big surprise for our families, a wedding without any of the rigmarole that so many of our friends had been through. But the champagne had eventually worn off and reality had taken its place, so we didn't get married that night. In fact six months had gone by and we still hadn't set a date. We hadn't even talked about setting a date. We'd get around to it someday.

But after four years together, I was ready to close the chapter titled "Free-Spirit" and start a new chapter called "Mother." I wanted to be responsible for someone other than myself and a twelve-cent goldfish. I wanted to have the needs of some small being be more important than my own. I wanted to share in raising a person to put out into the world, to take by the hand and teach everything I knew. I wanted a baby.

"Maybe your mother's right," I told Mark. "Maybe I am nesting."

He looked at me and his tanned face appeared to pale a shade or two. "Oh boy," he said.

I could have dropped the subject, knowing how he felt, but the force of motherhood pushed me on. "Maybe we should have kids," I said, "We'd be great parents."

He frowned at me. "We've talked about this. If we had kids, our lives would be over. Look at my sister. She and Tom barely get along; they have no life outside of the kids." He shook his head. "Everything would change."

I shrugged. *It would*, I thought, *but maybe it would change for the better.*

"And what about all the traveling you want to do?" he said.

"We could take them with us. Traveling is good for children. It exposes them to different cultures and makes them more open-minded."

He gave me a patronizing smile, as if he were the smartest and funniest man in the world. "I'd definitely have kids," he said, "if they could be frozen whenever we wanted to travel." Then he got up and walked away.

I was left sitting there with my answer and an image in my head of my laughing toddler suspended in a cryogenic storage tube. He was right, I supposed; having children would upend our lives, and we had good lives. We could come and go as we pleased, travel on a whim, have a carefree existence. We led an enviable lifestyle and I knew I was lucky, but the siren song was growing louder and I wanted something more.

I mentioned my plight to my friend Cassie one day. She nodded her head sagely and said, "I've been in that same situation. I kept thinking he'd change and he didn't. And then one day someone told me, 'It's not that he doesn't want kids, Cassie; he just doesn't want kids with *you*.'"

For a second her words rang in my ears and I scrambled through my Mark data trying to test her theory. He'd been besotted with his previous girlfriend; I'd met her once and could understand why. But she'd moved to Hawaii without him, married someone else and was trying to start a family. His first wife had left him too, remarried and now had four children. Clearly both these women had wanted children and he hadn't, ergo, it wasn't just me. Cassie's theory might have applied to her, but it didn't apply to me; the problem was definitely *him*.

    I wasn't thinking about taking matters into my own hands when I decided to come off the Pill—not exactly. "I've been on the Pill for 15 years," I explained to Mark, "and I'm just not sure it's the best thing for my body." I'd become more aware, since turning 30, of the things I put into my body. I conducted thorough research before taking medicines of any kind, and preferred natural remedies, when available. Using artificial hormones to trick my body into not conceiving didn't seem like a good idea anymore. Mark agreed, at least in theory; in practice there were issues.

    I wanted natural contraception, and so I studied my options and settled on what used to be called the Rhythm Method, which I'd always assumed had something to do with the speed and ferocity with which one had sex, but turned out to be all about synchronizing intercourse with the natural menstrual cycle. I understood the basics of reproductive science— sperm meets egg, etc.—but the book filled in the details that the school nurse, my mother, and even my high school biology teacher had all neglected to share with me. I learned about my reproductive cycle, how each month, my uterus builds a thick lining in preparation for a fertilized egg; then, once my ovaries are done ripening an egg, the hormone mixtures changes, the egg is released into my Fallopian tubes, and my body produces mucus to aid any incoming sperm in reaching their goal. If the egg isn't fertilized, the hormones switch again and begin the process of cleaning house and preparing for the next cycle. I had no idea all that clever stuff was going on in my body every month and it made sense why certain times of the month were fertile and others were not. But although the science of the method was logical to me, when it came to putting my absolute faith in it, I lost my nerve. I ran back to my doctor and requested a diaphragm and as much spermicidal cream as she could prescribe.

While my logical brain was calculating the dangers of getting pregnant unintentionally, the schemer in the back of my mind was doing the same math and figuring out the odds of conveniently having "a little accident." All I'd really have to do was neglect my diaphragm, leave it in the vicinity of a sharp object or two, or maybe just "forget" to use the cream. I wouldn't be the first woman to plan a devious pregnancy and I figured one of two things would happen. In scenario A, Mark would get the news of his impending fatherhood, throw a fit, and insist on a termination. I would defend my unborn child and deny his request. He'd see the error of his selfish ways, and ultimately stand by his woman. Once he saw his own eyes gazing back at him from our darling bundle of joy, he'd step boldly into the role of daddy and be the outstanding father I knew he could be. All's well that ends well. I get the baby I want, he gets the baby he needs, and his mother gets to say, "I told you so." We all live happily ever after. The end.

Scenario B was very similar, following the same pattern of receiving the news, pitching the fit, demanding and denying the abortion. It was the part where he looks into his baby's eyes that differed. In fact it wouldn't happen at all, because when Mark got the news, he'd hightail it out of town, refusing to acknowledge the existence of his offspring, or his (now ex-) fiancée. Forced to face the reality of raising a child alone, I'd scurry home to my mother in England, where I'd convert my former childhood bedroom to a nursery and my mother would spend her otherwise peaceful retirement caught up in a whirlwind of diapers, bottles, and teething gel.

I could have made either scenario work. I wanted a baby and it was going to take something drastic to make it happen. But what I really wanted was to do it right. I wanted to find Mr. Right, fall in love and, from that love, create a baby. I believed that Mark was Mr. Right, but if he didn't want children was he right for me? If he *was* Mr. Right, would I be okay not having children? Were my only options Mark or a baby, or was there some solution in between? And was I willing to do whatever it took to become a mother?

In the end, I couldn't in good conscience trick Mark into fatherhood. My desire for a child of my own was strong, but not so strong as to potentially wreck the lives of others, and not so strong as to risk an otherwise good relationship. I knew I'd have children one day; it was my destiny. So I waited. Mark's 40th birthday was on the horizon and a big milestone like that was bound to bring about a change of heart.

2
Destiny's Child
19 Years B.J.

Flashback to 1985 and times are tough for folks in northern England. It's the height of the Thatcher era; the once-thriving steel industry is on its knees, the coal miners are still reeling from a yearlong strike, and the outlook is grim for the working man. Even the joy of the national pastime has been marred by disaster— the Valley Parade stadium fire that killed 56 soccer fans, and the riots at Heysel, where 38 fans died. As if that isn't enough, British Telecom has announced it will phase out its famous red telephone boxes, and in a faraway land, an actor is now President. I'm 15 years old and added to the usual list of teenage angst is the AIDS epidemic and the threat of nuclear war. At least we have The Smiths to sing happy songs and cheer things up. Despite all this grim news, the air is crackling with excitement in a red brick, semi-detached house in the suburbs of Sheffield.

My sister-in-law Stacy rests one hand on her swollen belly and holds out the other, palm up, for my mother. I kneel on the floor and watch as Mum pushes her blue-framed glasses down to the end of her nose and squints at a needle. She pokes a length of thread through the narrow eye, makes a practiced knot, and smoothes the thread, dangling the needle just above the palm of Stacy's hand.

We wait.

Stacy and my middle brother, William, are expecting their first child. There's much to be done in preparation—a nursery to be painted, tiny cardigans and bootees to knit—so we need to know the sex of the baby. This calls for my mother's famous divining trick, tested and proven by my grandmother and undoubtedly by her grandmother before.

I glance at my brother. His dark moustache twitches, but his narrow, warm eyes—my mother's eyes—are trained dead on the needle. There's a tremble in the thread and the needle moves. Just a wobble at first, but then it swings in an almost imperceptible arc. We wait to see. How will it move? A circle? A line? There's a curve to its path, but then something happens. The needle seems to make a decision. It swings like the pendulum of my grandmother's old hallway clock, back and forth in long decisive strokes.

"It's a boy," my mother says, barely containing her excitement. She would have been just as excited had the needle predicted a girl.

A glowing grin spreads across Stacy's face. "I knew it would be," she says.

My brother nods.

Behind us, a rustling of paper lets us know that my dad has lowered the racing pages in order to watch. He says nothing, but I see his thin, smooth lips turn into a hint of his crooked smile. In a few more months, he'll have his first grandson and the Manterfield name will go on for another generation. None of us knows then that he'll have only two months in his new grandson's life. For now, everyone is excited about the coming new arrival.

My mother stills the needle and lets it go again. This time it moves in a wide smooth circle. Their next child will be a girl.

"That's what I'd want," Stacy says, "a boy and then a girl."

My mother sets the needle again to make sure she'll get her wish and nothing more.

My brother's smile has tightened. Kids are expensive, there's a brand-new mortgage payment and soon there'll be only one income to pay it. His beloved Ducati motorcycle won't be much longer for this world.

The needle doesn't move. It hangs as if bolted by some invisible device to the center of my sister-in-law's hand. There will only be two children. I can almost hear my brother sigh. Two is just the perfect number—a moderate number, enough to prove that they like children, but not so many as to appear common. A boy and a girl—just right.

"Do mine," I say and hold out my hand for my mother. My brother rolls his eyes. My mother does it anyway.

I hold perfectly still, the needle hovering over my palm. I feel a jolt—a tiny spark of electricity in the center of my hand—and the needle begins to move. A current prickles underneath my skin as the needle starts to sway, then something catches and it makes a wide circle around and around my palm. It tickles and I giggle; my first child will be a little girl, maybe one who looks just like me. My mum resets the needle and I watch again as it quivers and seems to choose a direction. It swings in a straight line this time—a boy. My mother resets again and the needle repeats the pattern—another boy. I grin at my brother. I've one-upped him already with my three children to his two, and matched my older brother, Ben, with his predicted three.

"I think that's enough," Will says, but Mum resets the needle anyway. *It* will tell *us* when it's time to stop. It swings in a circle—another girl—and I wiggle a provocative eyebrow at my brother.

"It had better not be for a long time," my dad grumbles. He doesn't know that I have a boyfriend who's two years older than me, but my dad needn't worry; despite my boyfriend's constant attempts at persuasion, my common sense (or fear of my dad's wrath or of a reputation as a slag) is winning the battle against my hormones.

When my mum resets the needle for the fifth time, it shoots like a laser beam from her finger and thumb, vertically down to my palm. This means there will be just four children for me. I don't know how the witchcraft works, if it works at all, but whenever there's talk of babies in our house, I ask my mum to test me, and every time my fortune is the same—a girl, two boys, and another girl. My brothers think it's all hocus-pocus, but I am certain I will have four children. I'm proud that I will have such a big family, bigger than our own family and bigger than those predicted for my brothers. I like being different, being contrary to the norm, and having only two children is so conventional. Having four children will be a statement of my individuality—too many to fit in a normal-sized car, too many to fit in a standard three-bedroom semi-detached house, and more than any of my friends' families have, except the Irish-Catholic family across the street. And twins run down both sides of my family, so I have no doubt that two of my children will be twins. Having twins will definitely be unconventional.

I always expected to have children, and not just because my mum's needle predicted it. I grew up in a time when that's what people did. They left school, got jobs, got married, and had families. On the quiet suburban housing estate where I lived, almost every family had children and every mother was at home to raise them. That's just what mums did. Every family had two parents and none of my friends' parents were divorced. That's just not what parents did.

I liked being part of a family. My immediate family comprised just three children, Ben, William, and me, but we had a large extended family—eight sets of aunts and uncles, 18 first cousins, and a rapidly expanding cadre of my cousins' children, the eldest being only four years younger than me. Our family tree looked more like the family English Ivy, creeping into every possible nook and cranny. Family weddings always included a photo of the entire brigade of Manterfields (or Bakers—my mum's side) stacked up on the church steps and stretched out across the forecourt. Ours wasn't a family that spent a lot of time together but most of my relatives lived in the same city as us, we saw my grandmothers weekly, and there were enough weddings, christenings, and funerals to make sure we all got together once or twice a year.

As the second youngest of my cousins, I had plenty of opportunities to be a bridesmaid when my older cousins got married, followed later by my brothers, who are 11 and 13 years my senior. I was there as, one-by-one, they married and had kids of their own, and I knew that my turn to join their ranks would come eventually. It wasn't until some years later, when my youngest cousin had her third child (the 39th child of that generation) and my oldest had her third grandchild (the 14th great-great grandchild) that I realized I was the *only* one of my generation who didn't have children.

My family might have been busy producing miniature people faster than a Mattel factory, but my friends were more like me. We had boyfriends, or sometimes just friends who were boys, but we also had plans. We were going to go to college, have careers, and distribute our talents around the world, far, far away from suburbia. After all, it was the mid-80s; our shoulder pads were getting wider, our hair was getting bigger, and our visions for the future were changing. Annie Lennox and Aretha Franklin were furrowing their brows and telling us how "sisters are doing it for themselves," stepping out from behind their men and stepping into the limelight, bold, strong, and taking no prisoners. Punk stars like Toyah Wilcox were screaming, "I want to be free, I want to be me," and I yelled back, "Me too!" *Flashdance* and *Working Girl* showed strong, beautiful (but approachable) women, the kind of woman I wanted to be, forging ahead, breaking down the barriers that society had set in their paths, and following their dreams. I wanted to be a welder; I wanted to dance like a maniac; I wanted to smash the glass ceiling and be a powerful but benevolent corporate superstar. But since that had all been done, I needed to find something new, some atypical career, something nice girls just didn't do—but nothing that would bring shame to my parents.

So I became a civil engineer.

I was good at math, liked building things, and most people I surveyed had no idea what a civil engineer did. When I told one elderly aunt I was going to be an engineer, she asked why on earth I wanted to work on a train. So I explained that civil engineers designed bridges and roads; they wore hardhats and pointed at plans a lot. The very best thing about my career choice was that girls simply didn't become engineers. I would be blazing a trail for countless young women in my wake. All I had to do was work hard and keep my eye on my dream.

They used to say that behind every great man, there's

a great woman, but I think that behind every great woman, there's a great mother, and my own mother cheered me on, all the way. She was a product of the grin-and-bear-it generation, those women who had seen the Second World War literally on their front doorsteps. The row of houses one street over from my mother's childhood home was bombed flat during the nighttime Luftwaffe raids on Sheffield in December 1940. She learned to accept whatever life dealt her and to be grateful. As a young woman, my mother had been accepted to the city's grammar school for girls, but later, she walked away from the chance of a career in science—a rewarding and uncommon career for a woman in 1950—to be a wife and mother. She told me she had never regretted her decision, but I could tell that she wondered what her life might have been like had she taken another path. At the age of 64, she obtained a Bachelor's Degree in Science from the Open University. She had no plans for a new career, but she got to hang her graduation photo on the living room wall. Who knows what great accomplishments she might have achieved if she'd begun 40 years earlier. She gave up that dream, but I wasn't about to give up mine, and I know she didn't want that for me either.

I had a clear vision of my future—jet-setting consultant, traveling the world, advising on dam projects in Vietnam, constructing international headquarters buildings in Hong Kong, and working *pro bono* installing clean water systems in sub-Saharan Africa. In this vision I had a house—a large brick colonial with shutters and a circular driveway—a moss green Range Rover, and a matching Barbour jacket. Somewhere in the picture was a faint glimmer of a husband, a kind, but ruggedly handsome man who worshipped the ground I walked on and shared the responsibility for our four children with the nanny and me. Although my dreams were adventurous and exotic, they never included me as a single woman, making her way alone; there was always a family in my picture. I didn't dwell on the details of who would raise my children while I was digging sewage trenches with the Maasai; the '90s were fast approaching, so I could have it all.

I was 16 when I first fell in love, not just puppy love or infatuation, but true gut-wrenching, hormone raging, wedding planning love. His name was Tim. He wore *Miami Vice* suits, had hairy bowlegs, and wiggled his slender hips when he danced. He loved his mum and his cat and, once he'd kissed me in the front row of *Top Gun*, he loved me, too. By the time Tim and I had celebrated our 18th birthdays together, we had plans to get engaged and had even picked names, Jennifer and Abigail, for the two daughters he wanted us to have (regardless of my mum's needle prediction). There was no doubt in our minds that we'd spend the rest of our lives together, so going away to the same college was a given. But when Tim didn't get accepted to my university of choice, I had to make a decision: follow my heart or follow my dream. The dream pulled hard, but the heart pulled harder and, in the name of love, I ditched my top-notch education and went with Tim to the small college where we'd both been accepted.

It took less than a month in the dreary town of Pontypridd—famous only as the birthplace of Tom Jones and home of what was once the world's longest single-span stone arch bridge—for my dreams to wake up and my heart to start getting fuzzy around the edges. Engineering superstars didn't trail around after men; they forged their own paths, even if it meant those paths weren't much more than single-tracks, just wide enough for one. I called the University and was told I would still be welcome, but I'd already made friends in Pontypridd—friends that I'd still have more than 20 years later—and I needed to make the best of the choices I'd made.

So, I broke up with Tim. I flung his broken heart aside and dead-bolted mine. I threw myself headlong into academia, blocking all thoughts of Mr. Right and making a project out of finding Mr. Wrong. I was good at it, too. There was the longhaired bricklayer, who would show up at my dorm room in the middle of the night, high and wanting to talk. He had a girlfriend and could barely string a sentence together, but he made me laugh and he loved to dance. There was the body builder with the glimmering blue eyes and the fractured but fun-loving family. He had no intentions of living anywhere but the tiny fishing village where he'd been born. My life as a fishwife? Not bloody likely. Jean-Michel, the over-emotional French road builder; Dafydd, the Welsh farm boy; and Alec, the most handsome man to ever walk the face of the earth, and the last of the Great Inappropriates. Alec had room for only two loves in his life—himself and his ex-girlfriend. Unfortunately, she'd gone and married his father, so would always be in the picture and I couldn't shake off the image of him in the throes of passion with his stepmother. Unavailable, unsuitable, or unwilling, there was no need to try to change these men; they were perfect just as they were—imperfect and so very wrong for me.

So, when my fledging engineering career led me to Los Angeles, I wasn't looking for love; in fact I'd sworn off men for good. In the back of my mind I thought that eventually, when the time was right, someone would come along and my destiny as I'd pictured it—career, house, husband, kids—would fall into place. I didn't expect I'd meet Mr. Right in L.A., where most of the men I encountered were either married-but-looking, gay, or so self-possessed they couldn't conceive of having a lesser human being such as myself anywhere near their personal space. In some cases, all three applied. Dating in Los Angeles was like a night out at *Cirque du Soleil*. There were so many fascinating tricks and talents, but sooner or later, you had to look away; it was just too bizarre.

So I wasn't looking for a husband, a boyfriend, or even a date when the backhoe operator on the construction project I'd been assigned to asked me if I'd like to go to Disneyland with his parents and kids. It seemed harmless enough, a free trip to Disneyland, with chaperones, but sometimes love sneaks out from behind a tree and comes at you like a crazed flying monkey. And if you don't have your wits about you, it will carry you off to a high stone tower, and then a would-be engineering superstar might turn down an international opportunity and wake up at 22 years old, married with two stepchildren, living in a long-stay motel in Palmdale, looking for a job that will get her home in time to make dinner. I know because it happened to me.

Suddenly, I was a wife and a part-time mother to two pre-teens. My weekends revolved around Chuck-E-Cheese and *Ernest* movies, and I mastered the art of refereeing battles for the remote control and mopping up tears. I found myself repeating all my mother's tried and trued lines, "I don't care who started it; I'm finishing it," and "Don't come crying to me when someone gets hurt." I was in the trenches, trying to make it through another weekend with the least amount of fighting possible, and when their dad started working extra overtime, I dug in for the team and did my best to make the arrangement work. It was so far removed from my vision of motherhood that I didn't even recognize it as the same thing. It wasn't until years later, after I'd left and my stepchildren had become parents themselves, that I realized I had missed an opportunity. But it was too late then. I was just relieved that my common sense had overcome my hormones and I hadn't brought more children into a marriage that should never have been. I wanted children of my own, but I wanted to do it right, at the right time, with the right man.

But when I hit 30, all that changed and the common sense/hormone balance tipped as if an elephant had sat on one end of it. Being with the perfect man was no longer a priority. I needed a decent fella to contribute some genetically suitable sperm and stick around to be a good daddy. Which is how I found myself weighing the odds of duping Mark—the duffel bag-toting, toddler-freezing adventurer—into parenthood.

On the surface, turning 30 was really no big deal. I ran a marathon that year, was catapulted into a new career in marketing (the problem with engineering being that it was full of engineers), and still got carded on a regular basis. But store clerks started calling me "Ma'am" instead of "Miss," my single friends were diving into marriage like lemmings off a cliff, and inside, my hormones were beginning to rage. My next big milestone birthday was just over the horizon, and even if life begins at 40, *new* life—a baby—doesn't stand a cat-in-hell's chance.

Statistics from the American Society of Reproductive Medicine paint a grim picture for the woman "of Advanced Maternal Age." The steady decline in fertility that begins at age 20 takes a dramatic dive south at age 35 and plummets like the first drop on a rollercoaster after 40. The chance of miscarriage is steady at around 10%, until age 35; by age 40, a woman has a 1-in-3 chance of losing a pregnancy. Down Syndrome rates increase almost tenfold between the ages of 30 and 40. And a woman who has not given birth by the age of 40 stands a 64% chance of remaining childless. But at that time, I was oblivious to all these details. I knew that getting pregnant would be harder the older I got, but I felt young and vibrant, certainly not someone "of Advanced Maternal Age." Still, my hormones were sending a clear message: if I was ever going to get *up* the stick* I was going to have to get *on* the stick.**

All around me, women I knew were joining The Mommy Club, that exclusive group whose membership all women are expected to covet. A membership card comes with all kinds of unique privileges, including special treatment in restaurants on Mother's Day, first dibs on days off at work, and the ability to voice an opinion on children, motherhood, child-rearing, or education, without being shot a sideways look of daggers and being told, "How would you know? You're not a mother." But the top membership perk, as far as I was concerned, was a baby, another human being to love and nurture, for the rest of my life. I wanted to join that club, and my body and society *expected* it.

When you're in your 20s, the standard icebreaker amongst new acquaintances is, "So, what do you do?" A conversation then ensues about career, accomplishments, and Great Moments in Corporate History. But once a woman hits 30, it becomes, "So, do you have kids?" It's as if what she does, her contribution to the world, her great achievements mean nothing if she hasn't produced a gaggle of heirs to replace her.

And this attitude doesn't just exist in suburbia, in the quiet rows of neat houses, dutifully washed cars, and landscaped front yards; it pervades every facet of society. One year, Mark and I went to West Hollywood, L.A.'s gay center, for the annual Halloween Carnaval, long before it became "The World's Biggest Street Party" and a tourist attraction to rival Disneyland. Late into the night we wound our way through the crowds on Santa Monica Boulevard, marveling at the creativity of the costumes, and watching the acrobatic sideshows, until our feet

British slang, meaning pregnant
**American slang, meaning to get busy*

yelped for mercy and we went in search of refreshment. We made our way into Starbucks, where a group of costumed revelers gathered for coffee. When Mark and I walked in, a man dressed in black rubber bondage gear turned and looked us both up and down. "Oh," he sneered through his rubber mask, "Breeders." I was too stunned to respond. There was no escaping the pressure from society anywhere, even among people who themselves shunned convention. If you were heterosexual, you were expected to breed.

Around this same time, something else was happening to motherhood; it was becoming glamorous. Stars such as Audrey Hepburn and Elizabeth Taylor had once taken short leaves from their careers to quietly produce babies before slipping back into the limelight as gorgeous as before. You'd see them cinched into tiny narrow-waisted dresses, waving from the red carpet of their newest movies—the ones where they play the slender, coquettish heroines—but news reports suggested that sometime during post-production they'd acquired children. But now, in the early 90s, celebrity moms were exposing their rounded bellies and parading their offspring like the hottest new accessory. When Demi Moore posed naked and seven-months pregnant on the front cover of *Vanity Fair*, the taboo of celebrity motherhood melted away. "You're either sexy or you're a mother," Moore was quoted as saying, and suddenly women could be both. Some celebrity moms, like Madonna, taunted the paparazzi by withholding pictures of their babies, but as motherhood became more accepted, celebrity babies became the hottest cover stories in town. A few years later, it was reported that *People* magazine paid $4million for shots of Shiloh, Angelina Jolie and Brad Pitt's biological daughter. J Lo and her twins scooped a cool $6 million, more than enough to decorate the nursery and pay for a lifetime of therapy. Suddenly, celebrity motherhood wasn't merely accepted, it was the New Big Thing. If being skinny, beautiful and glamorous wasn't enough for a woman to live up to, now she just wasn't cool unless she had an adorable toddler on one hip and a Kate Spade diaper bag slung across the other.

So where did all this leave a 30-something unmarried, childless woman who'd never owned a pair of Jimmy Choos? For me it meant showering buckets of maternal love on an unsuspecting goldfish and waiting for Mr. Right, Mark, to hit 40 and decide he was ready to be Mr. Dad.

3
Becoming Mrs. Fabulous
2 Years B.J.

I wasn't really surprised when Mark's 40th birthday came and went without fanfare, but I was still disappointed. There was no flash of lightning to bring about some miraculous change in his views on children and it was time to admit to myself that Mark wasn't going to change. He really didn't want kids, not even with me, and I had to decide what I wanted most from life. Was I willing to walk away from a five-year relationship and take my chances at finding Daddy Right?

I started paying close attention to men with young children, assessing them for other qualities to see if a man could be everything I dreamed of: intelligent and supportive, funny and kind, adventurous *and* paternal. As I conducted my survey, my list of requirements shrunk. A sun-bronzed Adonis could strut by me on the beach and I wouldn't even flinch, but a chubby hubby with a face like a bag of frogs could melt my heart with one smile if he had a toddler perched on his shoulders. Pretty soon, my list of desirable traits was down to one: paternal. While working on a play at a local theater I got into a conversation with a fellow actor after rehearsal one night. He was strait-laced, politically conservative, impossibly moody and smelled like an ashtray most of the time. But over drinks, he told me how he wanted to settle down someday and have a family. I hung on his every word like a lovesick puppy. By the time the bar closed, we'd settled on names for the two children we would someday produce together—Victoria for a girl and Robert for a boy—and I was convinced that this was the man I'd been waiting for all my life.

Later, when the vodka tonics and the taste of ashtray had worn off, I saw our future more clearly. Wanting to be a daddy wasn't enough to carry a relationship. But was *not* wanting to be a daddy sufficient grounds for dismissal? While my heart and brain battled it out, Mark and I limped along behind.

Swirling around in this stew of confusion was Jose. He was my boss at the local community bank, where I'd run the marketing department for the past three years, and during that time he'd become a good friend—just another nice guy among the great bunch of people I worked with. We'd go to the gym together, joined sporadically by other friends and coworkers, and I enjoyed spending time with him. He laughed at my jokes and had a quirky sense of humor. He referred to himself as Mr. Fabulous, and although it was meant to be tongue-in-cheek, I thought it suited him perfectly. During the time we'd known each other, we'd discovered so many unusual things we had in common. We both loved the old British Sci-Fi show, *Doctor Who*, and the Sci-Fi puppet show *Thunderbirds*. We also loved opera, mariachi, and Alanis Morissette. In fact, we had so many odd things in common that when he mentioned the collection of cuckoo clocks that his mother had repaired, I decided not to tell him about my own fascination, in case he thought I was making it up to impress him.

Over lunch one day in the spring of 2002, my

colleagues were talking about the pros and cons of dieting, and I chimed in with a story about Mark. I'd recently announced to him that I was going on a diet, but after only a couple of days I had crumbled and headed for my secret chocolate stash. When I lifted the lid, all the chocolate was gone and in its place was a post-it note with a cartoon drawing of a pig. I laughed when I told the story, but my friends sat silently; they were shocked. It was Jose who spoke first. "You deserve better than that," he said, "You're a catch."

I vaguely remember general murmurings of agreement from my other friends, but I wasn't listening anymore. I *was* a catch and I *did* deserve better than Mark. I deserved someone who wanted the same things I did and who would walk beside me through life to get them. I deserved someone who respected me, foibles, weaknesses, chocolate addictions, and all. I deserved someone who thought I was a catch.

The lighting in the restaurant seemed to suddenly change and the harsh glare of fluorescent took on a warm golden glow. All of a sudden I saw Jose, the funny little man I so enjoyed spending time with, with a new perspective. I saw his dark, gentle eyes looking at me with kindness and understanding. I saw his strong features—his fine cheekbones, strong nose, and thoughtful brow—and noticed for the first time how incredibly handsome he was. I saw his salt and pepper curls resting on latte-colored skin that looked sweet enough to eat. And I saw his soft, smooth hands—banker's hands, I'd always tease. They were the kind of hands a woman would want touching her skin. They were the kind of hands I could picture holding my newborn baby.

I avoided Jose for the rest of the day. I wasn't sure if I could look him in the eye without him recognizing something new in mine. My feelings of attraction were strong—not only lust, but something more. I tried to shake them off and made a mental list of all the reasons why I couldn't allow myself to succumb to this silly infatuation:

1. Jose was my boss, red flag, big no-no
2. He was 15 years older than me
3. He was two inches shorter than me
4. He had two grown children and was unlikely to want more
5. He was married (although word on the office floor was that they were separated, but still)
6. He was my friend and I didn't want to risk losing that friendship
7. *Everybody* liked Mr. Fabulous; just because he was kind to me didn't justify a stupid crush
8. He didn't own a passport and had never traveled farther than Mazatlán
9. He was obsessive-compulsive and prone to weird obsessions, such as collecting paperweights, knives, and cuckoo clocks
10. He was an organizational nightmare who could never find his glasses, frequently lost his car keys and periodically dropped his Blackberry in the toilet
11. He was my boss, red flag, big no-no!!

The fact that I was "engaged" to Mark didn't even make the list.

A few weeks after my "you're a catch" epiphany, Mark's mother came to visit from Northern California. "I'm going to spend the summer in Hungary," she announced, "and I want you to come with me."

She hadn't visited her homeland for over 25 years and she didn't want to go alone. Mark wanted to see his relatives again and the idea of traveling around a new country, staying in people's houses, and soaking up a new culture was exciting to me. I'd been trying to learn Hungarian, mainly to impress the future in-laws, but it was unlike any other language I knew so I hadn't advanced much beyond the basics and a couple of funny tongue-twisters. Total immersion would be the best way to boost my learning. But I was a corporate drone now and the most time off I could accumulate before the summer was a measly week.

"That's fine," Mark said, "I can't imagine spending the entire summer with my mother, either; she'd drive me crazy." As much as I liked them both individually, I knew how quickly mother and son could start butting heads, and neither would stand down.

We agreed that Mark would go with his mother for two weeks and I would join them in Budapest for the second week. I went to bed and left them surfing the Internet and haggling over the cheapest flights. In the early hours of the morning, Mark shook me awake. "We've found a great deal," he said. "The only thing is, I'll be gone for seven weeks."

I groaned and tried to force my eyes open. "Can we talk about it tomorrow?"

"We've got five minutes to book it or we'll lose the deal," he said. I pictured his mother anxiously waiting by the computer for my response. What was I going to say? *No, I won't let you go for that long.*

"Fine," I mumbled and rolled over. But I didn't go back to sleep. I lay awake, listening to them in the next room, excitedly planning their trip together. I was envious that I couldn't go, annoyed that I'd been pressed into a corner, but mainly sad that he was making plans— big plans—that didn't include me.

Mark packed his rolling duffel and left in April, right after my birthday, but I didn't spend much of the time he was gone alone. When Jose suggested we keep one another company over dinner one night, I was happy to accept. After that, we ate dinner together a lot, talking and telling stories. He made me laugh and I loved getting into a good debate with him. Sometimes he'd take a contrary corner just to get a discussion going. He never took offense if my opinions differed from his and I always walked away from our debates feeling just a little bit smarter. We began to get together on weekends, as well as weeknights, spending time browsing around bookstores and antique shops, or going for a run. We were just friends, hanging out together, but it seemed that neither of us had homes we wanted to hurry back to.

One night, in a conversation about Las Vegas, Jose mentioned his wife. I'd met her once, at a company event, and had found them an odd couple, completely mismatched in outlook, but somehow similar from almost three decades of association. I decided to grab the opportunity and ask the question that had been niggling away at me. "Doesn't your wife mind that you're never home?"

"I think she's happier when I'm not around," he said. He told me he and his wife had been living separate lives for years, still married out of habit, but completely disconnected. I felt a surge of excitement at the idea that he might be available and relief that I wouldn't really be breaking up a home if we did get together. This was all followed by a rush of guilt when I remembered my own home and the relationship I still had.

As my trip to Hungary approached, I resented having to leave Jose behind, but the talk of travel turned our conversation to the subject of our dreams. I told him I had a fantasy about hiking to the base camp of Mount Everest and that I wanted see the pyramids of Egypt and the Taj Mahal. I also mentioned wanting children someday. Jose's list included learning to surf in South Africa, drinking tea served by a Cha Walla in India, and learning to tango in Buenos Aires. He didn't actually believe any of this would happen. His wife's plan for them was to retire to Laughlin, despite the fact that he hated the desert. I went home alone that night with a fierce desire to make Jose's dreams come true—and to be there with him when they did. I felt a thrill of excitement when I pictured us together, beneath the magnificent minarets of the Taj Mahal, side-by-side on the famous bench where Princess Diana looked so forlorn, the hot Indian air clinging to our skin, sipping tea from a passing Cha Walla.

The night before I left for Hungary, I went back to the office after I was sure everyone had gone home. On Jose's desk I left a CD of tango music and a *Lonely Planet Guide to Buenos Aires*. It was a daring flirtation, thinly disguised as a hint for him to see his own dreams come true. Yes, I wanted him to be inspired, to throw caution to the wind and to book himself a flight leaving immediately for Buenos Aires. But the truth was, I wanted him to book two tickets—one for him and the other for me. I wanted him to rescue himself from his current life, and rescue me from mine. Because, when I thought about strutting around the floor of a smoky tango hall, held tight in Jose's arms, a shiver ran through my body and sparked every single nerve.

By the time my plane touched down in Amsterdam, my layover, I knew that I wanted to be on this trip with Jose, not with Mark. I wanted to explore the narrow streets of Budapest and linger in old cafes, sipping sweet Tokaji wine and letting the strange language of the people drift over us. I wanted to stroll through museums and gardens and go to the ballet or a play performed in a language neither of us understood. I wanted to savor the experience, soak in the culture, live for a little while as a Hungarian, with Jose. But all I could do was buy a postcard and try to describe for him the fields of multi-colored tulips I'd seen as my plane came in to land. I dropped it in the airport mailbox and reluctantly boarded my flight to Budapest.

Mark was waiting for me at Ferihegy Airport when I rolled my bag out of the arrivals lounge and on to the main concourse. His thin, wiry body hurried towards me and his narrow lips were pressed into an expression that told me he had a plan, that the best deals had been negotiated, and an itinerary for the week had been set. "We have to hurry," he said, pecking me on the cheek. "I think I'm parked illegally." I tried to imagine gliding around a tango hall in his arms, but tango is a dance of passion and, even after a month apart, there was none there.

Through the towns and cities of Hungary, in and out of churches and cafés, I tagged along behind Mark and his mother. They'd been traveling together for a month— the longest time they'd spent together in years—and their tolerance of one another was wearing visibly thin. I sat in silence in the backseat of their borrowed car, methodically erecting an invisible shield around myself and refusing to take sides. I gazed at the rolling hills of wildflowers while the two of them argued about routes. "I know best," his mother said and, instead of shrugging and letting it go, he argued back like a persnickety teenager. While they squabbled about where to have lunch, I would find a nearby gate and push it open to find an old cemetery or a tiny, immaculate flower garden. They fought about how to save a *florin* here or a *fillér* there and when they switched to speaking Hungarian, I melted even further into the background, glad that they'd forgotten I was there.

After three days we crossed the border into Austria, stopped in Vienna, and then headed to the tiny town of Melk to visit a magnificent hilltop monastery. Mark and his mother had been bickering since the early hours of the morning and I finally lost it. "Shut the fuck up!" I yelled. My expletive rattled around the tiny car, dinging off my fiancé and my would-be mother-in-law. They were stunned by my outburst, but all my pent up anger, my frustration with Mark, and my longing to be somewhere else, bubbled up and overflowed, and once it was out, I couldn't stop. "I'm so sick of listening to you two squabble," I said. "Why don't you just grow up?"

We drove in silence the remainder of the way and when I drifted away from them inside the monastery, neither of them bothered to come and find me. I wandered out to the gardens, through the roses and linden trees, thankful to be alone at last and grateful for the garden's tranquility. I had three more days with these people and then I could go home. But home was a place I shared with Mark and it was no longer a place I wanted to be.

I sauntered back to the Abbey and tucked in behind a German tour group. So far on the trip I had used my two years of high school German to find us places to stay, something to eat, and had even held a stilted conversation with a rosy-cheeked Austrian landlady, but the details of the Abbey's history were beyond the limits of my vocabulary and I let the group move ahead of me.

I don't know why I was drawn to the small wooden door in the side of a stone wall or what possessed me to ignore the No Entry sign, but I threw aside my usual respect for the rules and, when the tour group was out of sight, I eased open the door, swept aside a thick velvet curtain and stepped into a pink glow of light. I eased past stacks of dark wooden benches in what appeared to be a small antechamber, and out into the towering nave of a magnificent church. The early afternoon sun blazed through the windows in a cupola, reflecting off columns of deep rose marble and bathing the church in an ethereal light. Above me, the ceiling was painted with panels of frescoes depicting pink cherubs, their plump baby bodies flitting around stern-looking apostles. I felt my breath catch in my throat at the utter beauty of the place I had found. I wanted to stay there forever, bathed in the gentle energy of its sanctuary. I didn't want to be found; I didn't want my blissful tranquility disturbed ever again.

At the front of the church, an altar sprang up from the marble floor to the painted ceiling in an ornate column of shimmering gold. I stepped towards it, my neck craning slowly backwards to take in the awesome sight. At the top of the altar, I read an inscription, *Non Coronabitur Nisi Legitime Certaverit.* My high school Latin wouldn't stretch to reading the inscription, but a nearby sign gave the translation: "Without a legitimate battle, there is no victory."

I let out the breath I hadn't realized I was holding and I felt my shoulders sag. I had grown weary of fighting battles with Mark that I no longer wanted to win, but in that second, I knew that I would emerge unscathed to a new place where everything was beautiful and warm, and where my life would be filled with little pink cherubs.

Our final stop before returning to Budapest was Salzburg. I wanted to do the Sound of Music Tour (I had a secret yen to sing the "Do-Re-Mi" song on a hill overlooking the city), but Mark and his mother wanted to see the salt mines. We compromised, which meant that I never got to see the inside of Maria's former nunnery, but instead donned a hard hat and climbed aboard a rickety miniature train and plunged into the cold damp darkness of a mine shaft for half the morning. I kept calculating what time it was in L.A., trying to figure out when Jose would be up and have his Blackberry turned on. At the first opportunity after lunch, I made excuses about needing to shop for gifts and headed down to the

Getreidegasse, the old shopping street where Mozart was born. I found an Internet café, ordered a *Kaffee* so that I could use their computers, and logged into my e-mail account. With one eye on the street outside, I sent Jose a message. "Wish you were here," I typed, and waited.

Within seconds, a response came back. "I wish I was there, too."

I smiled and breathed a sigh of relief. It was good to be back in the company of someone I wanted to be around. I told Jose all about my hell, about what a fantastic trip it would have been if I hadn't been there with Mark and his mother. Then I told him I was looking forward to seeing him.

"I miss you, too," he wrote back. "Thanks for the CD."

I grinned with satisfaction and told him about the old wooden door, which, contrary to my usual tendency towards good behavior, I had crept through, and about the church I had discovered inside.

"Good for you for taking a risk," he wrote back.

Suddenly I was filled with a wave of even more foolish bravado. "Sometimes," I wrote, "you have to open doors, because you never know what wonderful things you might find."

It was a terrible flirtation, and I hoped I hadn't overstepped my bounds, but it had been fueled by a sudden sense of clarity regarding Jose. I hit the "Get Mail" button at least half a dozen times before his response came back.

"There are some doors that shouldn't be opened," he said.

My heart sank. Maybe he was right. He was married and, even if he was unhappy, it would be crazy for him to go fooling around with an employee. I wanted to be with him, but I wasn't willing to jeopardize his life or either of our jobs to do it. I would have to respect this and make no further move. I went to close down my e-mail. I'd been gone over an hour and it was only a matter of time before Mark tracked me down. My finger hovered over the mouse and my mind flashed back to the church. *Without a legitimate battle....*

Sod it, I thought, and typed one more message: "Some doors should be kicked down." Before I could get a reply, I saw the front door open and Mark came striding in, beaming at me.

"There you are," he said. "What have you been doing all this time?"

"Just checking my e-mail," I said, closing down the window and silently telling Jose good-bye.

Two days later, Mark and I were finally alone and I was finally going home. In the taxi on our way to the airport, he reached out and took my hand. "Sorry this wasn't the greatest trip for you," he said. "You know how my mother can be." I shrugged. "I've been doing some thinking," he went on. "Being around all my family like this, all my cousins and everyone, it's made me think that maybe it would be nice to have a little family of our own, you know?" I nodded my head, just a feeble movement. I *did* know how nice having a family would be. "I know it would mean some changes," he said, "some huge changes really, but maybe it would be worth it."

I forced a tight smile. This was the paternal equivalent of a summer vacation romance and, once we were back to reality, I knew the novelty would wear off. Plus, after the past week, his genes were the last ones I wanted to mingle with mine. I had thought that his only flaw was that he didn't want children, but even with that flaw so suddenly patched up, I could see that I had been so very wrong. "We can talk about it when you get home," I told him, but even as I walked through the airport departure gate, I knew that this would be the last trip Mark and I would ever take together and when I did have a family of my own, it wouldn't be with him.

Jose picked me up from the airport in Los Angeles. A brief e-mail from Amsterdam was all it took for him to offer to meet me. When I walked out of the Tom Bradley International Terminal and saw him waiting, he was like a ray of warm sunshine right to my soul. I wondered if we'd finish our e-mail conversation about kicking down doors, but he didn't mention it. He drove me to the company parking lot where I'd left my car for the week and, despite my jet lag, we sat in his car and talked for more than an hour. I told him I was going to start looking for an apartment; he offered to help me move. We talked until it was so late that I absolutely had to go, before my eyes wouldn't stay open any longer. I looked over at him and he gave me a smile that made my insides quiver. I was definitely home. In that second, I was certain I would kiss him. He could sense it too, I could tell, and he didn't back away. I sat for a moment, just looking at him, trying to keep my face calm, but inside, my mind was running all the computations regarding the consequences of leaning over and kissing my boss, my married boss. The desire to caress his plump, soft lips was overwhelming. I wanted to feel his salt and pepper goatee bristle against my lips. I wanted to run my hand across his chest and down the muscular thighs I'd so often stolen a glance at in the gym.

But I couldn't do it. I had made my decision about my own future, but I couldn't be held responsible for pressing him into his. Instead, I gave him a small smile and said, "Goodnight."

Safely in my car, I exhaled, forced my heart rate to

calm, and tried to disperse the long-ignored sexual tension that had built up inside me; it had almost crested the dam. When I glanced across at Jose through the two layers of car window, I saw him run his hands through his hair; the expression on his face summed up exactly how I felt.

I did finally get to kiss Jose, just a few weeks later. He'd booked a hotel room at the beach for a company event we were working and when he hinted that I should stay the night with him, I said I would. I packed a bag with three sets of possible nightwear—a midnight blue satin nightie, a cute pair of yellow babydoll pajamas, and a set of the most shapeless sweats I owned—still not sure how the evening would unfold. After dinner and some wine, I opted for the sweats, still mindful of our professional relationship. We leaned on the railing of our balcony, gazing out across the ocean and talking, and when he moved his face right up next to mine, I closed my eyes and kissed him. His lips were even softer than I'd imagined, more tender, and yet strong and firm. I felt myself drift away to somewhere I'd never been before, a safe place. I was reassured by the familiarity of kissing a very good friend, by the comfort of finally finding just the right person for me, and, when the tips of his fingers found a small exposed patch of skin beneath my ribs, I knew, without a shadow of a doubt and without compromise, that somehow this was the man with whom I would spend the rest of my blissful life. And this was the man with whom I would have children.

By the end of June I had moved into a new apartment with a friend, and on the Fourth of July— Independence Day—Jose told me that he was also making plans to move out on his own. After that, we spent almost every free moment together, so much so that my roommate nicknamed us Josisa. We had to catch up on so much lost time.

I was only mildly surprised when, a few months into the new stage of our relationship, Jose suggested not using a condom when we made love. We had been open about our previous partners and I knew that neither of us posed a health risk, but what about the risk of pregnancy? I had a flash of a vision of a dark-haired baby lying on my chest, with Jose looking proudly down at her, but my sensible side dusted her away. "I'm not on the Pill." I said.

"It's not a problem," he said, but then looked away. "I've had a vasectomy."

My world ought to have screeched to a halt right there. The list of all the reasons I shouldn't get involved with Jose had been shredded months ago, far outweighed by all the reasons I should, but I'd missed one very important point. It wasn't that Jose didn't *want* to have children with me; it was that he *couldn't*. Maybe I should have called the whole thing off right there and then, but I didn't. I was in love, so much in love, more in love than I'd ever been before. Jose was everything I had been looking for in a mate. He was kind and gentle, passionate and funny. He made me feel like I was floating on air and that anything was possible, so when he quickly added, "They can reverse it these days, you know," I believed him.

Less than two years later, we stepped up beneath an old wooden gazebo in Napa and became Mr. and Mrs. Fabulous. In the presence only of the Justice of the Peace and the witness we had shanghaied from the city office, Jose and I pledged to share our lives together, through thick and thin, come what may, for better or for worse. We spent our honeymoon in Rio de Janeiro, eating coconuts and cheese grilled on sticks, on Copacabana Beach, followed by a week in Buenos Aires, the capital of Argentina. In the *Lonely Planet* guidebook—the one I'd left on Jose's desk that night— I found what I needed. In an old hall above a *confitería*, just off the *Plaza de la República*, we paid our five dollars to a young Italian man, who used his best broken English to try to teach Jose and me to tango. We were terrible; I kept trying to lead and, instead of counting T-A-NG-O, Jose kept trying to count T-AN-G-O and stepping on my feet. But we laughed and vowed to find a better teacher when we got home. I was pleased to have helped Jose make one of his dreams come true; now I hoped that some simple surgery would make one come true for me.

4
Fuzzy Love

Doctor Abrams kept us waiting, so I passed the time by gazing around the examination room. My eyes flitted over posters and brochures for urinary difficulties, prostate issues, and kidney stones, but always came back to land on the plastic penis model. It came with interchangeable parts to show the difference between a normal prostate and the enlarged version and I was fascinated with the colored tubes that began in the testicles as a jumble of thin *capellini* pasta and joined somewhere on the way to the penis to become a thick strand of *bucatini*. I'd never paid much attention to the workings of the male reproductive system, and now I tried to imagine all this inside Jose and to figure out just where the cut had been made that prevented him from having any more children.

We'd found Doctor Abrams through the friend of the sister-in-law of a friend. Her husband had undergone a vasectomy reversal procedure and they now had a baby boy. A quick Internet search told us that the doctor was reputed to be one of the best in the field and, although some people might have tracked down every qualification, certification and recommendation he had, this one success story was all the recommendation we needed, and we were excited to meet him.

The doctor breezed in, all efficient business and no nonsense. With his grey beard and penetrating eyes, he reminded me of a serious Robin Williams. When he asked how he could help us, I suddenly felt like a child, waiting to tell Santa that I wanted a pony, when I knew my dad would barely concede to a goldfish. "I'd like a baby, please," sounded ridiculous, so I nibbled my lip and let Jose do the talking. The doctor nodded sagely as Jose explained our situation, and then he said he could help. He handed us a copy of a paper he'd authored for a medical journal, explaining his vasovasostomy procedure. He described for us the epididymus (the action tube) and the vas deferens (the exit tube) and how he would make a cut and rejoin the two ends of the tubes. "It's like sewing together two pieces of *vermicelli*," he said, using his own pasta analogy. I glanced at the penis model and the *capellini* and *bucatini* I'd noticed earlier and wondered if the doctor and I had some kind of psychic connection or if pasta was a universal simile for human innards. "Six to eight microscopic stitches in an area the size of a pinhead," the doctor continued. If his aim had been to impress us and convince us of his abilities, it worked.

"And what are the chances this is going to work?" asked Jose. "What are our odds?"

The doctor nodded again, as if agreeing this was an excellent question. "Patency rates, the odds of finding sperm in the tubes after surgery, are 80 to 90 percent. I've done many of these surgeries and the success rate is high. But there are several other factors to consider. For one, the older the vasectomy, the less likely the odds of finding sperm again. The testicles have effectively been shut down and it may take some time for them to start producing sperm again. Typically, in vasectomies less than ten years old, pregnancy rates are around 40 or 50 percent. How old is your surgery?" he asked Jose.

Jose didn't look at me. "About twelve years," he said.

I'd heard clearly everything the doctor had told me and yet I chose to disregard these particular statistics. Yes, the success rate lowered, but that was for other people, not for us. We weren't like other couples; it had taken us a long time to find one another and we were meant to be together. I hadn't had children up until this point because I was intended to have them with Jose. There was no question in my mind that, if Doctor Abrams could perform the surgery, Jose would produce sperm again. We were just lucky that way.

Maybe this kind of blind optimism was naïve, but it had served me well in the past. It was like filling in a sudoku puzzle in pen; there was no point starting it if you didn't believe you could solve it. Likewise, I wasn't going to subject Jose to surgery if I didn't believe it would be successful. And if Jose and I had been alone, I knew the opinion he would have voiced. He would have wiggled an eyebrow at me and said, "No problem; I'm Latin." Lucky, Latin, or just blinded by love, I heard what I wanted to hear and I knew that this would work.

"Now," said the doctor, "It could take up to six months for sperm production to resume. Then again, it could happen right away."

"That would be great," I said.

"I have to tell you this because you'd be amazed how many people get pregnant right away and then come in here and say, 'I thought you said it could take six months.'"

Jose and I grinned. We both knew we wouldn't be one of those outraged couples; we were planning on it working right away.

As the doctor led us out to make an appointment for

the surgery, he glanced back at me. "Have you had a full fertility work-up yet?" he asked. I shook my head. "I think it's a good idea," he went on, shuffling Jose's paperwork and passing us off to the receptionist. "You don't want to go through all this only to find out later there's a problem with you." He shook our hands and left.

Back at home I brought up the doctor's suggestion to Jose. He shook his head. "You're young and healthy," he said. "Clearly I'm the issue here. We need to try this first and then see what happens."

It made sense to me, but clear of the brisk efficiency of the doctor's office, other doubts began to settle in— not about whether the procedure would work, but about whether it was the right path to take. Was it really fair of me to ask Jose to go through this? To me, someone who'd never been under the knife, this was a major procedure, involving microsurgery and a general anesthetic. Jose was terrified of being put under and had asked the doctor if the procedure could be done using a local anesthetic, but the doctor had explained that it was vital the patient was completely still.

That night, as we ate dinner beneath our apricot tree, Jose asked the question that had been swirling, unformed in my head. "What if I don't wake up again?" he asked.

"You don't have to do this, you know," I said. "We could find another way. Or we could adopt; I've always thought I would adopt." In more recent years, my fantasy of motherhood had evolved to include adoption. I felt that the socially responsible thing to do was to produce replacements only for my partner and me, and then provide a loving home for an adopted child—or two, if my mother's needle prediction held true. I had once met an amazing woman who chose to have only one biological child and then adopted five more children from all over the world. She had inspired me to follow her example.

"I'd be open to adoption." Jose said, "In fact at one time it was part of my plan, too, but I want you to have the experience of being pregnant. If there's a way we can make this happen, I want you to have a baby of your own first."

I nodded. This was what I wanted, too, and I was grateful that Jose was willing to go through with it. I was proud of him for facing his fear and agreeing to the surgery; I was in awe that my desire for motherhood meant so much to him, and I felt a glow of tenderness that he loved me enough to do this for me. I knew that it wasn't just that he wanted more children; he wanted more children with *me.*

Before dawn on the morning of the surgery, three months after our wedding, I went with Jose to the hospital and waited in the family area while he was taken away and prepped. I looked around at all the other people waiting. Some looked sick, some limped, all looked as though they needed the surgery they were about to have. My husband didn't need to have his surgery; he had elected to go through it for me. I felt a pang of guilt and a creeping sensation of fear. I thumbed through a dog-eared *Reader's Digest* and tried to think positive.

After what felt like hours, but was perhaps 30 minutes, the receptionist let me in to where Jose lay in bed, dressed in a blue surgical gown, while a gaggle of young nurses prepared him for surgery. Jose was smiling and I was glad to see he was in good spirits. When one of the nurses secured a blue shower cap on his head, Jose grinned at me and I was grateful for his permission to laugh. A few minutes later, a distinguished-looking white-haired gentleman came by and introduced himself as the anesthetist. He had a kind, gentle face and a manner perfectly suited to bouncing giggling grandchildren on his knee or administering carefully calculated doses of anesthetic.

"You know," he said to Jose, "I started a second family when I was in my fifties."

"Is that right?" said Jose.

"Yep. Best thing I ever did," he said and gave Jose a firm, manly smile. Suddenly I felt confident that Jose was in good hands and that this decision would prove to be a good one for us.

Satisfied with Jose's vitals, the anesthetist explained what would happen and that the operating room would be kept cold to reduce bleeding.

"Great," said Jose, after the team had moved on. "I'll have a bunch of pretty young nurses staring at Little Elvis and the Twins and it's going to be ten below zero in there. They're all going to wonder how I snagged myself a gorgeous young wife."

I squeezed his hand and gave him a wink. "Don't worry," I assured him, "they'll just assume you're rich."

He laughed and I squeezed his hand a little tighter, and then it was time to say good-bye. I kissed him lightly on the lips and watched as the nurses wheeled him away.

With Jose gone, the air in the room seemed suddenly smothering. I tried to take a deep breath, but the air wouldn't fill my lungs. I pushed my way out of the room, down the quiet carpeted hallway and finally out into the fresh morning air. Suddenly, my head was filled with sobering thoughts. *What if something goes wrong? What if it isn't successful? What will I do if Jose dies?* And what was I going to tell his family? They didn't know he was having surgery today. He hadn't wanted them to know, figuring he'd wait until I was pregnant before explaining how it had come about. If anything happened to him, it would all be my fault. Suddenly I wanted to run back inside the hospital and tell the doctor I'd changed my mind. I wanted them to hand over my husband so I could take him home with me, safe and sound. More than anything else, more than the desire to have children, I wanted Jose to be okay.

My first instinct was to call my mother, not because I wanted to talk about my feelings, but because I *didn't*. Although my mum and I are the best of friends, we never talk directly about matters of the heart. I knew she wouldn't ask me if *I* was okay, so I wouldn't have to tell her that I wasn't. She would be strong and pragmatic, and so I'd be strong and pragmatic, too, even if my instinct was to cry like a little girl.

From my hometown 6,000 miles away my mother asked all the right questions. "How long will the surgery take? Will Jose be able to go home today?"

I took courage from her composure and calmly explained that Jose would be about an hour in surgery, a few hours in recovery and that I would be able to take him home that afternoon.

"Let me know when you hear something," she said. I promised that I would, and hung up, grateful for her strength.

Back in the hospital I tried to pass some time. I walked the hallways, looking at the artwork, and then drifted to the cafeteria and forced down a bagel and coffee. Finally, there was nowhere else to go but back to the waiting room to wait. I took a seat in the corner and opened the mystery novel I'd picked up in the gift shop downstairs. Every few minutes, I glanced at the clock, took a sip of water, and went back to the exact same sentence in the book. The room was filled with other families waiting for their loved ones, some of whom were probably seriously ill. I was determined to keep Jose's surgery in perspective and not agitate the others by pacing up and down the floor.

At 11:20 Doctor Abrams popped his head around the waiting room door and caught my eye. I searched his face for any indication of his news, but the man was a professional, his face a mask of discretion. He led me out to a quiet corner of the corridor and finally cracked a practiced smile.

"Jose is in recovery right now," he said. "The surgery went well and the tests showed the presence of semen."

I didn't know whether to laugh or cry, hug him or shake his hand. I wanted to do all of them. I wanted to skip down the hallway and tell everyone what an amazing husband I had, how much I loved him, and that soon, very soon, we were going to have a baby!

5
A New Woman

The waiting room at my OB/GYN's office was full, as usual, with young women, mothers with small children, and expectant mothers in various stages of pregnancy. I was there for my annual checkup, but I expected to be back within a matter of months to confirm my pregnancy and begin prenatal care. I slid into a seat amongst the mothers, already disassociating myself from the younger women and aligning with the women with children. I felt more mature suddenly, as if I'd passed a milestone and into a new realm of responsibility. I had graduated to become a woman who was trying to get pregnant. I was ready for this new chapter in my life, ready to take on the challenges, and ready to build a life with Jose and our children.

While I waited, I ruffled the pages of *Parenting*, barely scanning the pictures, and looked around the waiting room, trying to elicit a smile from any of the young children. If I could get one of them to smile back, it would prove that I would be a good mother, the kind of mother that children were drawn to, a *natural*. When a flossy-haired girl tottered over in lilac-colored soft shoes and bared her single tooth at me, I smiled back tenderly, feeling the warm glow of maternity spread through my body. There was no doubt in my mind: I was going to be good at motherhood.

I surveyed the other women in the room, analyzing them to determine the kind of mothers they were or would be. I knew I wouldn't be like the axe-faced mother, screaming like a banshee at her ornery little demons, nor would I be an over-protective mother, padding the world around my child so that he would never have to experience anything unpleasant. I'd be a firm mother, determined to raise children that could be let out in public without embarrassment, but my children would never want for love or affection. I'd be an open-minded mother, introducing my children to a broad range of people and experiences so that they could form their own opinions based on experience and not prejudice. I would feed them healthy food, but not have a meltdown if their grandpa took them out for a hot dog. Oh, I would definitely be a good mother.

I glanced at the two noticeably pregnant women in the waiting room and imagined myself sitting there a few months from now in some cute little maternity outfit, my firm belly peeking out over the top of my yoga pants. I would definitely be that kind of pregnant woman and not the sort to wear a pink flowered potato sack and sausage wrapper leggings.

The nurse practitioner—a kind, attentive woman— called me in and asked me if I was still in the same relationship. With a slight air of smugness, I told her that I was now married. I waited for her to ask the usual slew of questions about monogamy and practicing safe sex, but she didn't. She just assumed that because I was married I wasn't sleeping with anyone else and that neither was my husband. It was a reasonable assumption in our case, but it struck me as odd compared to the grilling I would have received before we'd tied the knot. It was interesting how much a single piece of paper changed my standing.

"And are you using contraception?" she asked, again without the lecturing tone I always heard as an unmarried woman. I remembered our last meeting when I'd felt embarrassed explaining that Jose had had a vasectomy and that we weren't using other contraception. She'd given me a sideways glance and I'd felt the need to quickly explain Jose's and my sexual histories, so she didn't launch into her spiel on the dangers of sexually transmitted diseases. This time I stammered for a moment before telling her we weren't using contraception as such, and then explaining the whole story of Jose and his recent surgery.

"Oh," she said. "I hope it all works out." She gave me a reassuring smile and instructed me to lie back. I put my feet in the stirrups and wriggled down the table, wondering how long it would be before I'd be here again.

Six weeks after his surgery, in the cramped bedroom of our cramped beach cottage, Jose and I made love for the first time since his reconnection. I was as nervous as if it had been the first time ever. Sex wasn't just for fun anymore—it was for babies.

In my years before Jose, every time I had sex, I'd thought about the consequences if my birth control failed. I'd read the fine print on my packages of pills and condoms and studied the effectiveness rates. The Pill was 99% safe and condoms 98%—assuming perfect use. But I wasn't perfect. Pills got skipped, condoms malfunctioned, and those statistics soon lowered so that the possible 8% failure rate could easily have included me. After a few days or weeks of sweating the outcome of each contraceptive disaster, I'd breathe a sigh of relief when my period finally arrived thinking, "I got lucky." An unplanned pregnancy would have been an unwanted pregnancy.

But all that was about to change. Now, at 34 years old, for the first time in my life I was going to make love and *hope* it would result in a baby. I was about to commit to a lifetime of responsibility.

"Are you sure you want to do this?" I asked Jose. "It's not too late to change your mind." My asking was more a formality, rather than an actual opportunity for him to cop out. There was no turning back now; we had already crossed that invisible line. Now we were going to make a baby.

Jose felt different when we made love now. His skin was softer than ever before and every place I touched him sent a jolt of electricity through my fingertips. His gaze was fierce, and he held me closer to him than I'd ever been before. We were a united front now, heading out together on our journey towards parenthood. It was going to be a wonderful trip.

The next two weeks seemed to pass in ultra-slow motion. The sensible side of me was being realistic, knowing there was little chance that Jose would have sufficient healthy sperm so soon after the surgery, but the dreamer in me was hoping for a miracle. I fantasized about sending Doctor Abrams a bottle of champagne with my positive pregnancy test tied around the neck.

We had promised each other to be realistic and not get excited until we were sure the surgery had been successful, but one night the subject of names came up and we launched headlong into a discussion about what to name our baby.

"I like traditional names," Jose said, "And I'd really like to choose a family name."

I agreed and we ran through all our relatives, trying

on their monikers. I pictured walking to kindergarten with little Leslie or Ernest, named for my father or grandfather, but those were antiquated names, not at all appropriate for my mischievous, dark-haired, little boy. Jose suggested my brothers' names, Ben and William, but I didn't know how I would choose one over the other without causing a family ruckus.

"My favorite uncle was Valentino," Jose said.

I'd heard lots of stories about Uncle Tino over the previous few years. "Wasn't he the drunk?" I asked.

"He liked a drink now and again, yes."

"He's the one you said used to ride the rails then show up periodically at your house for three squares and some money?"

"Uh-huh."

"Isn't that the uncle who was in San Quentin?"

This time Jose only nodded.

"And you want to name our first-born son after him?"

Jose took a defiant stance. "He was funny and I really liked him."

I mulled Valentino around in my head. The name meant brave or strong and I conjured up images of Rudolph Valentino gazing out from beneath his *Sheik* costume with those startling eyes and fine chiseled features. My little boy might not look like *the* Valentino, but he would be handsome and just as charming, like his daddy. Jose has what he likes to call the profile of an Aztec Prince, the one seen in pictures, standing atop a pyramid with a stunning and perfectly formed sacrificial virgin draped across his smooth, manly chest. Jose has the strong, slightly hooked nose and broad brow of his Mexican ancestors, coupled with his mother's delicate bone structure and slightly paler complexion, inherited from her French father. Someone with a taste for that look—me, for example—could easily describe him as devastatingly good-looking and there was no doubt in my mind that our son would be a lady-killer, and well-suited to the name, Valentino.

Jose pulled out some old yellowed photographs of his relatives.

"See the green eyes," he said, pointing to a handsome young man with neatly combed black hair and luminous eyes. Even though it was a black and white photo, it was clear that those eyes weren't the dark brown of the other family members or even the mysterious blue of the one blond uncle; these eyes were clearly green, the kind of mesmerizing green of a mountaintop pool.

Jose gave me a look that sent a tingle like the brush of fingertips all the way down my body. "How would you like it if that gene popped up in our little boy?"

I felt my chest tighten and my face flush. "I'd like that a lot," I said.

We settled tentatively on Valentino or Francis (Frankie) in honor of Jose's uncle and my maternal grandfather, and for a girl, Sophia for my grandmother, and Victoria for his, holding our mothers' names, Margaret and Matilda, as potential middle names in the event of twin girls. We made a pact not to share the names with anyone and not to make our final decision until we met our new baby. It was fun having a secret and I was excited for our future.

The week before my period was due, I woke up feeling not quite right. I didn't want to say the word out loud, but what I felt was nausea—not sprint-to-the-bathroom, collapse-on-the-tile nausea, but a definite queasiness. My breasts felt different, too. They were heavy and seemed fuller than usual, and my arms kept brushing along the sides of them whenever I moved. Within a couple of days, they felt like two pulsating watermelons and I knew I was pregnant.

Jose and I walked to a local diner for dinner that

night. It was a little over a mile, but it felt like ten to me. When we finally arrived, I collapsed into the red vinyl booth and scanned the menu. I was starving, but nothing looked good. I ordered a large bowl of minestrone soup and when it arrived I dug into the accompanying saltines.

Jose looked over his patty melt at me. "Are you okay?"

"I don't know," I said, wondering if I should share my suspicions with him, or if I was just being silly.

"Do you feel ill?"

I shook my head. "Just odd."

I couldn't use the word *nausea* because I didn't want to get his hopes up, but I told him all my other symptoms. He nodded his head sagely. "Let's wait and see," he said, but I saw a smile slip onto his lips.

I thought it was too soon to be showing symptoms of pregnancy, but once back at home I scanned the Internet for information. Although morning sickness wasn't expected to appear for two to eight weeks, tingling, tender, or swollen breasts could show up "as early as a few days after conception." I chose to ignore the part that mentioned other possible reasons for these symptoms, such as impending menstruation or emotional stress. I was seeing what I wanted to see—again.

The next day I headed to the drugstore to purchase a pregnancy test. There were so many tests to choose from. Some had pink lines—two for pregnant, one for not; some showed a plus sign or a negative sign. There were digital or not digital with Yes/No or Pregnant/Not Pregnant display options. Some offered testing earlier than any other brand; others offered a faster testing time. It was overwhelming. I wanted to choose the best test; I wanted to get my results as early as possible, with the minimum hassle. I wanted it to be accurate, but most of all I wanted it to show a positive result.

I was shocked to realize that I'd never had cause to buy an at-home pregnancy test before. I'd had two pregnancy scares that I could remember. The first was with my first real boyfriend, when a condom had burst and he'd gone with me to the clinic in town, where the nurse had prescribed an emergency morning-after Pill. My second scare was in college when I was taking my final exams and had been too busy and stressed to notice that my period was late. I was a day away from taking a pregnancy test when my period came. Since then, I'd either been smart, careful, or just plain lucky, certainly luckier than some of my friends.

I chose a test that promised accurate results up to four days before my period was due and took it to the cashier, placing it boldly on the counter. The young woman rang it up and smiled at me. "Will it be good news?" she asked.

I felt myself blush and smile. "Yes," I said, but as she was making change and bagging my purchase, I thought about how I would have felt if a positive test *wouldn't* be good news. What if I'd been terrified about the outcome of the test? What if I was facing single motherhood, or an unsupportive partner? What if an unexpected pregnancy was the very worst news I could imagine? Or what if a negative test result would be the end of my world? It was so rude and inconsiderate of her to ask such a prying question, but none of those situations applied to me, and so I let it go.

At home I laid out the necessary tools: clean plastic cup, test stick, step-by-step instructions with diagrams. I scanned the instructions. Morning urine is best, it said, but I couldn't wait another day to find out. Jose wasn't home and, although he knew I had my suspicions, I hadn't mentioned taking the test in case he thought I was crazy. Maybe I was. My period wasn't even late yet and the doctor had warned us it was unlikely to work the first time, but I was filled with hope and the expectation that things were bound to go right for a couple like us. We were lucky people, the kind of people for whom things always worked out.

I'd already come up with a plan for how to tell Jose our good news. I would buy a can of Chef Boyardee ABCs and pick out the letters to spell "I'm pregnant" and then serve them on a piece of toast for dinner. I also knew that once I saw a positive result, I wouldn't be able to contain myself long enough to even make it to the grocery store. More likely I would run around the house like a lunatic and then calm myself down for long enough to call Jose and scream, "Guess what?"

I perched on the toilet seat and followed the instructions, starting my flow of urine and chasing it around with the cup until I captured a reasonable measure. I dipped the tip of the test into the warm liquid for the prescribed amount of time, replaced the cap, and waited.

I picked up a newspaper from the basket beside the toilet and attempted to fill in a couple of numbers on the day's sudoku, but I couldn't concentrate. I peeked at the test. One line. *That's good.* It meant it was working. Applying the "watched pot never boils" theory, I got up, washed my hands, and went to find the cat. I dangled a toy mouse for her; she gave it a nonchalant pat with one paw and went back to sleep. I went to check if the mail had arrived; too early. I filled the kettle to make tea and checked the clock again. It had been the longest three minutes ever, but finally it was time. I picked up the test and looked at the results window.

One pink line.

I checked the instructions again to make sure what one line really meant. It meant I was not pregnant. I stared at the window on the plastic stick, trying to see if maybe there was a second line that was just too faint. I couldn't see one. I scanned the instructions for all the reasons I might have had a negative result. My period wasn't due for another two days so my hormone levels would still be low, probably too low to register on the test. I didn't use first morning urine, so that might have affected the results, and I'd drunk a lot of water that morning, which would have definitely diluted the hormone levels. What's more, I'd read on the Internet that false-negative results were common—more common than a false-positive. I decided I would retest in a couple of days and kicked myself for not buying a two-pack.

Two days later, before I made it back to the store to buy the second kit, my body showed the ultimate, indisputable symptom of a negative result—a period. I had been as regular as clockwork since the age of 12, and here I was, 22 years later, regular still. I used to be relieved whenever my period came, glad I hadn't been included in those contraceptive failure statistics, but that had been when I was a different woman. Now, I was a woman trying to get pregnant, and the sight of the blood made me feel as if my body had let me down.

I tried to convince myself I wasn't sad, wasn't bitterly disappointed. I tried to pretend I hadn't really believed we'd be lucky enough for it to work the first time. I put on a good show by laughing at myself for jumping the gun, and then I told Jose and confessed to taking the test. He gave a sheepish smile and admitted that he'd been hoping it had worked, too. He pulled me into a tight hug and held my head against his shoulder. "I'm sorry, Baby," he said. "Maybe next time."

6
The Aztec Prince
& the Weird Childless Aunt

Iknew my biological clock had clicked into overdrive
when I risked the wrath of my sister-in-law for sex. It
was almost noon on a hot, dry Saturday in October,
six months after our wedding. The tender vegetable
plants in my garden had wilted from lack of water and
our street saw a steady stream of fishermen and
beachgoers in search of elusive free parking. Felicity, my
cat, had staked out a spot at the foot of the bed to ensure
maximum airflow from the ceiling fan above and refused
to move, despite the waves that Jose and I were
generating across the mattress.

It was the wedding day of Teresa, Jose's only niece
and his only sister's only daughter. We had no role in
the wedding ceremony, but it was the first big family
gathering since our own wedding and I wanted to make
a good impression on Jose's family. Unfortunately, we
were also in the Hot Zone—the window of three or four
days around my ovulation, when we had sex at every
available opportunity— and wedding or no wedding, we
couldn't miss the opportunity to try again for a baby.

Mission accomplished, we made it to the church with

barely two minutes to spare, our faces still flushed. Forced to park in the farthest corner of the crowded lot, we jogged to the church, trying not to break even the slightest hint of perspiration. I patted down my hair and rounded the corner to the church's front entrance, and there she was—my sister-in-law, Yolanda. She turned her mascara-laden eyes on us and narrowed them into dagger-like obsidian slits. "You're late," she said and my stomach shrank to the size of a petrified walnut.

As Jose's second wife, I had stepped carefully into my place in the family. I was careful to not storm in with a "new sheriff in town" attitude, assuming everyone would fall in love with me. I'd bided my time, allowing his family, especially his son and daughter, room to get to know me. My tactic seemed to have worked. His parents had taken to me immediately, and I to them, and I had a cool but mutually respectful relationship with his children, Penny and Scott. But Yolanda was proving to be an impossible iceberg to melt. It wasn't me in particular she didn't like—she didn't seem to like anybody. But she was Jose's only sister and would be the only blood auntie to my children. Even if we'd never be great friends, I wanted us to get along so my children could have a good relationship with their aunt.

It was tough, though. She bordered on frigid with me, never made eye contact, and certainly never spoke to me directly. She lived in the house on the same lot as Jose's parents and, as the side gate was usually locked, accessing their house meant passing through hers. Her coolness towards me made our otherwise enjoyable visits to his parents uncomfortable. But I was determined to wait it out until she finally thawed. Our tardy entrance to the wedding wasn't exactly the step forward I'd intended.

The church was already a murmuring mass of women in big hats, small boys in clip-on ties and shiny shoes, little girls in frilly dresses, and at the altar, the nervous-looking groom. I couldn't remember which side of the church was for the bride, but three rows from the front, on the left I spotted Scott, Jose's son. I grabbed Jose's hand and slid into the end of the same pew, just as the organist struck up the first chords of the Wedding March. I turned and grinned at Jose to let him know that all was well, but his expression was strained. "You okay?" I whispered. He nodded and turned his eyes to the back of the church, where the bridal procession had started. I turned back the other way and smiled at the woman next to me, recognizing her face, but unable to pinpoint her in the few members of Jose's family I'd met. Then it dawned on me who she was.

It had been almost five years since I'd seen her at the company dinner—the only time we'd ever met. She was slimmer now and her hair had been cut and highlighted, but I realized—from the tension radiating from the bodies on either side of me—that in my haste, I had sidled up beside Jose's ex-wife. And there I sat with my husband to the left and his ex-wife to the right—a painfully blushing rose between two thorns.

It was the first time Jose had seen her since he'd moved out of the house more than two years before and I couldn't help but wonder what thoughts were going through his mind. Was he reminiscing about the good times, or remembering the worst and thanking his lucky stars he had left? I felt a twinge of envy that she had been his wife before me. I tried not to picture her as the young pretty blonde she had been when she and Jose met. I tried not to imagine him in love with her, and I tried not to wonder how he'd felt when his son was born, and then his daughter. But it was like trying not to think about elephants; the more I told myself to push them out of my mind, the more the images paraded past. He'd been young when his children were born and he'd admitted he hadn't been ready to be a father, although he had stepped up to the role and he loved his children dearly. It would be different with me; he wanted to have a baby with me and was willing to do whatever it took. But I couldn't help but envy the woman who had already borne his children.

I wondered how she saw me. Could she see, if not openly acknowledge, that I was a nice person, that Jose and I were well-suited, and that she was much happier now that she could live her own life without him dragging her down? I scoffed at my own precious naïvety. More likely she considered me a brainless floozy who'd caught her stupid husband in his midlife crisis and wrecked the plans for her golden years. As the ceremony began, I cast sly sideways glances, taking in her pretty flowered summer dress and small pearl earrings and questioning my decision to go with a flowing sapphire-blue Chinese pant suit and silk brocade Doctor Scholl's. I had wanted to wear something conservative, nothing short or low-cut, but I suddenly realized that I wasn't going to blend into the woodwork in this getup, or any other for that matter.

It was strange to sit among Jose's family and picture this event as if I hadn't been there, as if things hadn't changed. But they had changed and he and I were forging a new path together. At a similar gathering next year, we might be sitting with a new member of our little family. What would everyone think of that? Jose's mother would be pleased and would welcome her newest grandchild; his father would be confused for a while, but most likely slap his son on the back and say "God damn!" once he figured out that his grey-haired son was a daddy again. His ex-wife would piece together the puzzle quickly and probably think he was a stupid old man; it would be strange and awkward for Penny and Scott to have a much younger half-sibling, but they were both reasonable adults and they would come to accept him or her. As for Jose's sister, it was anyone's guess how she might react. She loved children and I'd seen her melt into a cooing, beaming, teddy bear whenever a baby was around. Most likely, she'd insinuate herself into my child's life and take over as doting aunt, but probably see me as no more than the producer of her precious niece or nephew, still not a sister. Regardless, we had decided not to tell his family that we intended to have children, and as nobody asked, there was no reason to tell.

As the wedding procession began, I cooed along with the congregation at the adorable flower girl and stifled my reaction to the oh-so-pregnant matron-of-honor, wondering if she would make it through the entire ceremony without going into labor. Jose's niece looked lovely, walking down the aisle to marry her childhood friend who had waited so patiently for her to see him as something more. She was the image of her mother, but with softer features and what must have been her father's personality. It made me wonder what had happened in Jose's sister's life to make her into such a hard woman.

Jose had been the firstborn and only son of his parents and his mother adored him. He joked that his feet hadn't touched the ground until he was five and that his mother had pre-chewed his meat until he was twelve. He wasn't serious, but I wouldn't have been surprised if it was true. Fifty years later, he could still do no wrong in his mother's eyes. In addition, he was the only male in his generation and consequently the apple of his uncles' eyes and the center of attention among his older female cousins, who had doted on him and treated him like their own living doll. Six years behind him came his sister, just another little girl, and Jose speculated that her current attitude had stemmed from that early envy.

He was the Aztec Prince; she was the Aztec Prince's kid sister.

After the mercifully short ceremony, the bridal party gathered in the afternoon sun and Jose was immediately whisked off for family photos. I stood by myself in the forecourt, upset that I hadn't been included, and uncomfortable standing alone, but relieved that Jose's ex-wife wasn't in the photos either. I was rationalizing that I ought to let it go, because I was the new wife and maybe the family was uncomfortable because the old wife was there and they didn't want to hurt her feelings, when I was surrounded by a flash of color and was suddenly lost in a swirl of swishy fabrics, clanking bangles and sparkly eye makeup.

"You must be Lisa."

"We've heard all about you."

"We're Tony's cousins."

It took me a second to realize that Tony is Jose's middle name, and the name his family calls him, and that these were the cousins he had grown up with and told me so much about.

"I'm Sandi. I'm the oldest," boomed the one who was a dead-ringer for her mother.

"I'm his cousin Marti."

"I'm Maria."

"We call her Tilly," said Sandi.

"I'm Niña."

"She's the baby," Marti chimed in.

"I love your outfit," said Niña.

I gathered myself up in the melee and stared at the four women who surrounded me. They were of equal height, like dolls in a series, but all with different features. Taken individually, they weren't at all alike, but seen as a group, they were obviously sisters. I knew these women from the countless stories Jose had so affectionately told me. As girls they had lived with Jose and his family for a while. Marti was the one who had owned a pink '57 Chevy with a record player on the floor; Tilly and Niña had taught him to do the Mashed Potato and the Twist; Sandi was always the one holding him in his baby pictures.

"We grew up together, you know," said Niña.

"He was such a spoiled brat," Marti piped in.

"He was always getting into trouble," said Sandi. She threw back her head and let out a loud cackle. It was clear that these four women had adored Jose, and still did. I got an immediate image of Jose as a small boy, his hair neatly combed to one side, with that mischievous twinkle that had never left his eyes. It was the same cheeky face that I pictured whenever I thought about how my little boy might look. I could imagine them spoiling him rotten. "Welcome to our crazy family," Sandi said and grinned at me.

I smiled and for the first time that day, I felt as if I might actually belong.

The reception was held in the south ballroom of Luminarias restaurant on a hill overlooking Los Angeles. The room was a glittering array of pink tablecloths and burgundy trimmings, with each table adorned with an elaborate silver pedestal topped with a shower of pink stargazer lilies and dark red chrysanthemums. I sniffed the air for the aroma of standard wedding rubber chicken, but instead my nostrils picked up the nourishing scent of sizzling steak fajitas, refried beans, and the unmistakable aroma of fresh homemade tortillas. Suddenly I was starving.

After everyone was seated with their food and the DJ had made an announcement requesting that no one steal the centerpieces, the mariachis arrived and struck up *Guantanamera* while the guests joined in the chorus between mouthfuls of dinner. As the players wandered between tables serenading guests and taking requests, an elderly man removed his jacket to reveal a dashing set of striped suspenders, and requested *Cielito Lindo*. Everyone cheered and joined in with *"Ay, Ay, Ay, Ay."*

At the bridal table, the groom requested *Sabor a Mi*. The bride blushed as the guitarist plucked out the opening notes and the guests let out a universal "Ahh."

When the troupe made their way over to the table next to us, a beaming woman with cheeks the color and shape of Fuji apples, and a dress and figure to match, took the DJ's microphone and requested *Volver*.

"Oh boy," said Jose as a collective murmur of approval went around the room. I turned to question his reaction, but the accordion and trumpet players struck the first aching chords of a love ballad. I felt a chill run up my neck and goose pimples spring up on my skin as the singer gave a moan of anguish. The DJ reached for his microphone, but the apple-cheeked woman clutched it firmly in her plump hand and with a voice that could shatter cheap glasses, she closed her eyes and sang as if her heart was about to break. Hers was a loud, coarse and out-of-tune rendition, but no one seemed to care. As she reached the chorus, everyone in the room joined in with a passion I'd never seen before. I craned my ears to listen to the words of the chorus, and come up with an approximate translation.

"What are they saying?" I whispered to Jose.

"*Volver*," he said, putting his hand over his heart and turning dreamy eyes to me. "Return, come back to me."

I smiled and looked around the room at the weary faces lost for a few moments in memories from long ago. Maybe they were thinking of their own weddings or of loves lost, but more than one pair of eyes was full of tears and my own throat had squeezed almost closed. I felt a great affinity for these passionate, uninhibited people. They were Americans, but they had not forgotten where they came from and embraced the traditions of the generations that had come before. I wanted to adopt this culture and be included in its traditions. I wanted my children to be raised around these people.

In my own family I was always the odd one out. I was the kid sister, younger than my two brothers by more than a decade, who blazed her own trail and never looked as if she'd settle down. No one ever seemed surprised when I did something unconventional. They didn't blink at my choice of mismatched partners or my decision to move to another country. They had come to expect the unexpected and I was always happy to deliver.

My dad had been the traditionalist in the household, the rule maker and enforcer, the governor of great British propriety and expectations. My brothers came to adulthood under that reign and followed traditional routes. They chose careers and stuck to them, married suitable women who were good for them, and went on to celebrate their silver wedding anniversaries. They bought houses in nice neighborhoods and produced wonderful children who have (so far) made it to adulthood without being arrested, publicly humiliated, or disowned. My dad would have been pleased with the way they both turned out. But a month away from my 16th birthday, on the cusp of adulthood and at a time when I was struggling for a grasp on adult independence, I was freed of those constraints by my father's untimely passing. So I rebelled against the norm, bucked expectations and forged my own path, which is how I came to be the Weird Childless Aunt.

The Weird Childless Aunt is an odd creature in literature, in film, and in real life. Sometimes she's portrayed as the irresponsible Auntie Mame, sometimes she's the hard-edged, but softhearted Auntie Em, or she's even the dippy, but lovable serial killer, the Abby or Martha Brewster in *Arsenic and Old Lace*. Simultaneously envied and pitied, she's the rolling stone, free to roam the world, to quit a job for a tentative but exciting opportunity, to go to a concert or a midnight movie on a whim, to load up a backpack and climb a mountain. But she gathers no moss, no security, no stability, no cozy family life. It's sad that she'll have no children to see her into old age and carry on her family line. I was only 34 years old but, aside from poisoning gentlemen callers, this was me.

I wanted to be a good role model for my nieces and nephews, but when my brother or sister-in-law would say that my middle niece was "just like her Auntie Lisa" I got the impression that they saw her as inheriting all the worst qualities of her Weird Childless Aunt. They cited her stubbornness, flightiness, or moodiness as evidence, but to me those traits looked like determination, adventurousness, and creativity, so whenever they compared her to me, I'd grin and respond, "Lucky girl." And whenever I saw any of my nieces and nephews opting to take the road less traveled, I hoped that their Weird Childless Aunt had somehow influenced them.

But the main problem with blazing your own trail is that people become skeptical. Because I didn't follow the prescribed path, I think my family assumed I was lost, that I'd never settle down, and that I had no interest in having children. That wasn't true. I wanted to be an equal in the family, to move beyond my role as baby sister. I wanted to host the big family Christmases at my house, instead of spending Christmas at someone else's house where there were children. I wanted the family tree on my Mum's living room wall to be taken down so my children's names could be written in. I wanted to be able to turn to my mum for her advice on taking care of my baby and be able to see her holding my child with the same expression I'd seen when she'd looked at my brothers' children—a look of real caring and the promise of never-ending love. It was fun to be different, unique, and a wayward influence on my nieces and nephews, but I still wanted to belong.

My brothers and I have a weird childless uncle, my mum's baby brother, Uncle Alan. Uncle Alan is not actually weird; he's just not like my other aunts and uncles. He always had a tan and drove natty Triumph sports cars. He traveled to interesting places and took stunning photographs with a very expensive-looking camera. My other relatives had noisy homes with overstuffed floral couches and souvenirs from English seaside resorts; the home he shared with my grandmother had deep leather wing chairs and shelves of books and was so quiet that you could hear the old grandfather clock tick-tocking out in the hallway. Our Christmas trees were strewn with gaudy baubles and paper ornaments we'd made at school; his was a work of art with carefully placed porcelain dolls in Victorian dresses that my grandma said I could touch as long as I put them back in exactly the same place.

I liked my uncle—he gave me my first bottle of real perfume—and as an adult, I felt an affinity with him because he wasn't like his siblings. But then he was diagnosed with Huntington's chorea, a degenerative disease with no known cure. His lifelong friend had recently died and he lived alone. With no children to take care of him and see to his affairs, the task fell to my mother and her sisters, already in their 70s. They moved him from his beautiful three-story house into a nursing home where he would have 24-hour care and some company, so he wouldn't be alone. Watching him grow old was heart wrenching. It made me realize that there were selfish reasons for having children, too. People with children had someone to turn to as they aged. People with children had a built-in community of support. People with children didn't die alone.

I wanted children because I wanted to have the experience, to have laughter in my home and have the adventure of raising human beings, but with a husband 15 years my senior and a family halfway around the world, what would become of me in my old age if I never had children? I had created an image of myself in my 90s, pruning my roses in a cottage garden overlooking the Pacific Ocean, going in for a cup of tea and a sit-down, and quietly passing away with my cat in my lap—it was a picture that suited me just fine—but what if I got sick? What if I became incapacitated and spent my last years in a home? Who would come to see me? Who would manage my affairs? The importance of family and a community of relatives came into sharp focus.

If Jose outlived me, he'd have his children and perhaps grandchildren to take care of him, but they'd be under no obligation to take care of me. A secure old age wasn't reason enough for having children, but it was certainly a consideration. I wanted a family, I wanted to be a part of Jose's family, and I wanted to graduate from my current status as Second Wife and Weird Childless Aunt. I wanted to belong.

It was only two weeks after Teresa's wedding that we were at another family wedding. All the same family guests were there, but this time, I was the wife of the father-of-the-bride and could not have been more uncomfortable in my role. I was very grateful that Penny had included me in the wedding party—and even in the wedding photos—when she could have easily chosen to keep me on the sidelines, but another part of me would have been happy to just keep a low profile. This time I chose the dullest, most conservative old lady suit, a kind of muted potato sack that touched my body only at the shoulders and covered me to my wrists and ankles. Even so, as I was escorted down the aisle by a groomsman to the front row of seats, I felt the eyes of the mother-of-the bride's friends and family burning into the back of my head. Nonetheless, I held my head high and for a fleeting instant I was glad I was not yet pregnant.

As father-of-the bride, Jose was in constant circulation, being pulled here and there for fatherly duties. I stood aside from the main action and kept smiling, determined to show no fear, even if I would have rather been anywhere else in the world. I scanned the reception for a familiar friendly face—any familiar friendly face—and was relieved to see Jose's younger cousin, Niña, on the far side of the room. I strode boldly past the table of "friends of the mother-of-the-bride" and smiled in their general direction, trying to keep my legs from shaking and wobbling around like Jell-O. I passed the table of "family of the mother-of-the-bride" and did the same, thinking how sweet it would be if the patterned carpet opened up and swallowed me whole, depositing me fully intact to the safety and comfort of my home. But then I would probably be accused of creating a stir and trying to steal the limelight—the very last thing I wanted to do.

I was glad for the safe haven of Jose's cousin, finally feeling comfortable for the first time all day. But eventually she had to leave to make the long drive home and Jose was called up for the father-daughter dance; once again I was alone at a table for eight. I felt like an island in the center of the room, surrounded on all sides by the wagons of the enemy, and it seemed as though every hostile eye in the room was trained on me. I wanted to go home, but I couldn't. I had to stay and enjoy the party.

When the DJ announced the cake cutting, a crowd of people gathered around the bride, the groom, and the cake, but I decided to stay where I was and just smile inanely. I watched for a few moments until a wave of courage flooded over me. I was allowing myself to feel like a leper and yet I'd done nothing against these people. My only crime was to fall in love with Jose and he had fallen in love right back. As his wife, I had every right to be there and to enjoy the festivities. And what's more, my paychecks had helped to pay for their steak dinner. I grabbed my camera and elbowed my way into the midst of the cake-cutting crowd.

When I headed back to my table, Jose was in the middle of what appeared to be a deep, personal discussion with his sister. I slowed my pace, not wanting to intrude and not wishing to have my newfound elation deflated by a cold shoulder from Yolanda. I was trying to decide whether to go somewhere else and wondering where that could possibly be, when Yolanda cocked her head my way and appraised me with her dark piercing eyes. "Are they treating you okay?" she said.

I wasn't sure what she meant at first, until I glanced around the room and realized she meant "them"—all of them.

"Because if I hear that anyone's been mean to you," she went on, "I'm going to start breaking glasses."

My sister-in-law has a deep scar across her nose and cheek. According to Jose she'd been caught in a bar with another woman's husband and hadn't been quite quick enough to dodge the broken bottle. While she'd driven herself home that night, the other woman had left in an ambulance, so when Yolanda said she would start breaking glasses, it was not a turn of phrase; she meant it.

I nodded and tried on a friendly smile. Then I looked her dead in the eye. "No worries," I said. "It's good."

"Alright then," she said. "But if they start anything, just let me know." She gave me a faint smile and for an instant I saw behind the mask to the woman who loved her family fiercely. She left the table and I sat for a moment, stunned. Once the shock of our interaction had passed, I swelled with self-satisfaction. I had earned a valuable ally and I felt as if I had cemented my status in the family, even though it was still not clear what had brought on this change.

On the drive home, Jose and I finally got some time alone and I asked what had changed in Yolanda. "When you elbowed your way into the crowd for the cake cutting, you showed courage," he said. "You got in there with the enemy and told them, 'Screw you, I belong here.' She respects that."

I was part of his family now and my children would not only be loved and cherished, but they would be protected with a passion. My only remaining concern was to make Jose a daddy again before his daughter made him a grandpa. It would be too weird for a child to be an aunt or uncle, especially to an older niece or nephew, and it would be too weird for Jose to have to take his children *and* his grandchildren to the park. Hopefully, I'd get lucky—and soon.

7
What a Wonderful World This Would Be

I love the old Sam Cooke song, "Wonderful World," so much so that I began to work on my own version:

Don't know much about biology,
Don't know much about fertility,
Don't know much about appointments to make,
Don't know much about what pills to take.

It was November and I still wasn't pregnant. At Jose's six-month follow-up appointment, Doctor Abrams informed us that Jose's sperm count was low—2 million per milliliter, when it should have been 20 million, and that his motility was sluggish, and his sperm somewhat misshapen. Despite this picture of gloom, the doctor's recommendation was merely that we wait, insisting that these results should continue to improve with time. Again, he suggested I get a fertility workup. Again, I told him I would, and again I left with no intention of doing so.

It wasn't that I didn't believe him, or even that I refused to admit that I could be to blame for our inability to conceive. The fact was, I had no clue what a fertility workup was, or how I should go about getting one, and I was too afraid to ask. Doctor Abrams threw out the term so easily, as if it was something I should know all about, and I was embarrassed that I didn't know something so fundamental about my body.

I tried to spot the gap in my education that would explain why I didn't know this. I'd grown up with brothers and, because of my original choice of career—engineering—most of my friends had been male. I had girlfriends now, but none who'd had any difficulties in getting pregnant. In fact, my friends who had children mostly fell into one of two categories—those who decided to get pregnant and just did, or those who didn't decide to get pregnant but did anyway. My guess was that, even if I asked my friends, most of them wouldn't know what a fertility workup was either. Fertility issues weren't something that was readily talked about and I felt better knowing that most women didn't come with this information pre-loaded; it wasn't passed down from generation to generation. Doctor Abrams had been using the term for so long, he'd most likely forgotten that it wasn't a part of most people's daily vocabulary. It was old hat to him, but I was stepping into a whole new realm, a foreign land way beyond anything I'd picked up in biology class or on my day-to-day travels as a woman. I'd spent almost 20 years trying *not* to get pregnant, and had been very successful. I had never thought of getting pregnant as something you *tried* to do; it was just something that happened when you stopped trying *not* to. I was heading out into uncharted territory and I was scared.

I examined what I *did* know about fertility and infertility and came up with a handful of experiences. I had been eight years old when Louise Brown, the world's first test tube baby, had been born less than 40 miles from where I grew up. I remember seeing pictures of the squashy-faced baby all over the newspapers and trying to understand, with my 8-year-old knowledge of babies and science, how they'd managed to grow an entire baby in a test tube. Louise Brown's name stuck with me over the years and I came to understand that she had been conceived through *in-vitro* fertilization, now commonly known as IVF, and that her successful birth had spawned a revolution in fertility treatments for women. But this was a medical miracle, a rare occurrence and I certainly didn't know anyone who had undergone such treatments.

Then I remembered my friend Chris. In my early 20s, I'd had a group of married friends in their 30s, the oldest of whom had been trying for a number of years to have a baby. I knew she'd "had problems" but I'd been raised not to ask personal questions, especially in the realm of "female troubles." I knew she'd undergone treatment and that the calendar in her kitchen had three days of the month circled with red marker and that this was the cause for some sage nodding amongst the girls and some hearty elbow nudges among their spouses. I knew she'd suffered a string of disappointments and that it had been a long and painful process for her, but I didn't know any details. She eventually had a baby girl, who was now around five years old, but our relationship had dwindled to an annual holiday card with the little girl's photo, and I was none the wiser for her experience.

But once Jose and I confided in close friends and relatives that we were trying to conceive, everyone seemed to have war stories and advice. Almost everyone knew someone who had experienced fertility issues, who had maybe been through treatments, taken fertility drugs, undergone IVF, had a healthy baby, had an unhealthy baby, had four babies at once, adopted, or given up and bought a puppy. I took some comfort in the fact that we weren't alone, but also felt a growing sense of anxiety that the odds of us being unable to conceive might be higher than I'd initially imagined. If infertility was such a common problem, maybe it could happen to us. I did a bit of digging around on the Internet and quickly discovered that it already had. While the general consensus was that a couple was considered infertile once they had been unable to conceive after a year of trying, for a woman my age— almost 35—it was only six months. It had already been six months for us, so technically we were considered infertile. That's when I started digging in earnest.

My trip to the bookstore was supposed to be a covert operation. I was uncomfortable telling Jose I was going to shop for books on how to get pregnant. It seemed that procreation was such a natural thing that millions of people did without effort, not the kind of thing you needed a book to explain, but I was beginning to realize that I didn't know what I didn't know. Maybe there was something obvious we were overlooking, and maybe just a tweak in diet here, a small lifestyle change there, or some nifty new technique was all we would need to make this work. I didn't want Jose to feel responsible for our problems—even though his slow, deformed, thinly spread sperm could barely limp the few inches to my eggs every month—and I wasn't about to start playing the blame game. We needed to maintain a united front and solve the problem together, as a team. Even so, I went underground on my mission to find my answers. Unfortunately, Jose insisted on coming along.

I managed to shake Jose off in the bargain book section of Barnes and Noble and slipped upstairs. I'd already been to the pregnancy section on a previous visit, not long after Jose's surgery, when I was convinced I would get pregnant right away. I'd bought the requisite copy of *What to Expect When You're Expecting* and spent a pleasant afternoon terrifying myself about all the things that could go wrong once I was actually pregnant. Reading that book was almost enough to put me off reproducing forever and I thought, for the sake of the continuation of the human race, that it ought to come with a warning. But the book didn't have much to say about how to get pregnant in the first place, so I bypassed the pregnancy section of the bookstore and made my way over to health.

I browsed through the various illnesses and syndromes looking for a section on fertility. It wasn't until I turned into the next aisle of books covering women's health that I found what I needed. The little white sign on the shelf was jarring: Fertility/Infertility. It showed, literally, the fine line that exists between being able to conceive and not. And the section didn't contain just a book or two, or even a full shelf. I was confronted with an entire bookcase devoted to the subject. There were books about choosing the baby's sex, dealing with polycystic ovarian syndrome, and meditating through infertility. Others covered fertility diets, Chinese medicine treatments, IVF, and a mysterious thing called GIFT, which I thought might be another ailment, but turned out to be the procedure of placing unfertilized eggs and sperm into the fallopian tubes instead of a Petri dish. It was overwhelming. I thought about my new version of *Wonderful World* and added several extra verses listing all the things I didn't know much about.

Don't know much about endometriosis,

Don't know much about Gamete Intra-Fallopian Transfer...

Finally I found a book about preparing for pregnancy. It covered all the basic information I'd already learned about the reproductive system, plus a list of all the ducks I'd need to get in a row before getting pregnant, and a rundown of possible problems when things didn't go as planned. I checked the index and found there was an adequate section on improving sperm quality, and a list of tests that might be included in a fertility workup. I took the book, passed through the Fiction section and grabbed a copy of the next Jasper Fforde *Thursday Next* novel I'd been wanting to read, and went in search of Jose.

I found him in the magazine racks, leafing through a copy of *Bicycling* magazine.

"Find anything interesting?" he asked.

I shifted the novel to cover the pregnancy book and did a strange head-bob thing that was neither a nod nor a shake. Then, feeling guilty and ridiculous for being so secretive, I ducked my head and showed him the books.

He glanced at the pre-pregnancy book and nodded. "Good idea," he said.

I smiled at him and wondered why I had felt the need to be so secretive. He wanted me to get pregnant just as much as I did. Why wouldn't he want me to get as much information as possible? And why was I so uncomfortable about him knowing? It wasn't a secret that we were going to need some help. He was completely supportive about us having children together. He'd been willing to undergo surgery so that I could have a baby, so he certainly wasn't opposed to doing whatever it took to make this work. I realized my resistance had nothing to do with him and everything to do with me. I wanted to be perfect. I wanted to be a great mother, and a great wife and partner, and I wanted to make everything simple for Jose. I'd created a vision of what it would be like to be a mother and a vision of what it would be like to try for a family. My vision was made up of romantic nights and tender love, of little blue lines in test windows and announcements with pasta shapes. I had imagined a phone call to my mother that started with the words, "I have something to tell you. Are you sitting down?" and I'd pictured strolling around Babies R Us, while my friend Lou pointed the handheld scanner at all the practical things she'd know I'd need and I pointed it at anything cute. My fantasy hadn't made concessions for abnormal sperm morphology, fertility workups, and undercover investigations. It was apparent that getting pregnant wasn't going to be as simple as I'd hoped— and I didn't like that.

Back at home, I flipped open the book and skipped over all the stuff I'd been doing since before Jose had his surgery—quitting caffeine and alcohol, taking a daily prenatal vitamin, etc.—but I stopped short when my eyes caught sight of a section that made similar recommendations for expectant fathers. I looked over at Jose, sitting peacefully on the other couch, blissfully unaware that I was now armed with information, with all barrels trained on him. I tried to sound casual.

"We need to drink less coffee," I said.

Jose put down his magazine. "Says who?"

I pointed at the book. "It says here that 'the time it takes to conceive may increase with paternal caffeine intake above 700 mg per day.'"

"How much is that?"

"Five cups of coffee, maybe six. Small cups."

He thought about it for a moment, and then shrugged, "I could switch to decaf, but not in the mornings."

"And, of course, I need to quit drinking, too," I added, hoping he'd take the hint that *I* meant *we*.

"What? Totally?" His interest suddenly went from piqued to panicked.

"That's what it says here."

He put the magazine away and put on his serious face. "Do you know how many babies are conceived after a night of boozing?"

"I know, but…"

"Does it mention in there how stress affects the

ability to conceive?"

"I haven't got to that bit yet." Or more likely I'd skipped over it in my haste to find tangible solutions.

"We just need to eat right, drink coffee and wine in moderation, and most of all *relax*."

I sighed. "Okay, but can you empty the cat box from now on? It says here I could get toxoplasmosis."

His face formed into a mask of tolerance. "Fine," he said. "I'd be *happy* to do that."

I'm sure he thought I was being neurotic, but I didn't care. I was on a mission to figure out why I wasn't yet pregnant and it was clear to me that I was going to have to take charge. Pregnancy wasn't just going to happen for us; we were going to have to make it happen, and if that meant giving up some of life's luxuries, such as coffee and wine, we were *both* going to have to sacrifice.

I'd never paid attention to pregnant women before, in fact I'd made a point of not staring, but suddenly I seemed to be surrounded by them and I succumbed to a severe case of belly envy. I noticed every detail about the pregnant women I saw. I watched how they walked, their backs arched and hips thrust slightly forward. I noticed when their hands subconsciously ran over the gentle curve of their bellies. I paid attention to how their partners looked at them, at how close they stood together, and I tried to imagine how it would feel to carry another human being inside me. I felt like one of Charles Dickens' wretched orphans, pressing my sooty nose against the window of a tall Georgian house, peering in at the occupants gathered around a crackling log fire—the sweet girl with pale ringlets and a velvet dress, the little boy, a miniature copy of his proud father, and the mother, doing her needlework and watching demurely over her brood—while I stood outside and watched and waited to be let inside.

And it seemed that the more I longed for admittance,

the more those around me got their tickets to the Mommy Club. It began with my employees, the year Jose and I were married, and quickly spread to my friends, then finally to my own family. The previous year, on my annual visit home to England, I had admired my brother and sister-in-law's new minivan and joked with them that the seven-seater allowed room for them to add one more child to their existing four. I had been met with laughs and a stern glare from my brother, but when Christmas rolled around, their card to us was signed from "Ben, Lorraine, Leslie, Peter, Jane, James and...?" A switch in brand of birth control pill and misread directions had resulted in the conception of my youngest niece, Alice. My mother's needle trick had proven fallible for both brothers and was no longer looking so promising for me.

All my research had suddenly made me something of a fertility expert, in my mind at least, so when Melissa, a newly married coworker, announced that she had come off the Pill to "see what happens," I felt it my duty to take her aside and explain that sometimes these things could take time and that she shouldn't be disheartened if it didn't happen right away.

"Not always," piped in my colleague and good friend, Lou. She and her husband had tried a similar experiment and a month later found themselves sitting in their motor home in Yosemite, drinking rum and cokes and staring at a positive pregnancy test.

Although Melissa was young, she had not created an environment in her body conducive to conception. She was overweight, seldom exercised, drank copious amounts of alcohol, and used high caffeine energy drinks to recover. She also thought nothing of popping a Vicodin for a headache, something that would have knocked me to the ground and kept me there for days. As I had been following the advice of my assorted books and medical advisors and had been living a clean life, I couldn't help but feel a "holier-than-thou" attitude towards Melissa's self-assured flippancy.

The following month I arrived at work and immediately sensed a prickle in the air. I looked to Lou for a clue, but she averted her eyes and seemed suddenly quite busy.

"I have news!" said Melissa, bounding from the kitchen and I knew what was coming next. "I'm pregnant!"

I felt the color drain from my face and then immediately flush back in. "That's great," I said, trying to control my voice and sound happy. I *was* happy for her, because I knew it's what she wanted, but I couldn't help but feel angry—and humiliated. And I felt something worse, too—a sense of desperation and perhaps a foreboding destiny.

It wasn't fair that she'd become pregnant so easily; she didn't deserve to have it be so simple. But life, I was learning, isn't fair. I was embarrassed that I'd played the sage and advised her based on my own experience. I was coming to realize that my own experience was the exception rather than the norm. For the first time, I thought that perhaps I might never have a baby, at least not "the old-fashioned way." But now wasn't the time or place to start entertaining such thoughts.

"So," I said, with as much joviality as I could muster, "how far along are you?"

"Four weeks." She giggled.

I stared at her. *Four weeks?* That's so early. How could she be announcing it to the world when so much could go wrong? At only four weeks, how could she even be sure?

"I know," she said, as if reading my thoughts, "but I just had a feeling, so I took a test and it was positive, so I took another and it was positive, too. I couldn't believe it, but I went to the doctor's this morning and they didn't even want to do a test so soon, but I insisted and it was positive! I was so shocked!"

After she had left for the day, presumably to call everyone she knew, Lou finally made eye contact with me. "I'm really sorry," she said.

I wasn't sure exactly what she was sorry about, sorry that it had happened, sorry that I'd had to hear all about it, or sorry that it wasn't me. "It's okay," I said, which seemed to cover all the possibilities.

"That should be you," said Lou.

I nodded. She was right, it should be, but it wasn't.

"It's not fair," she said.

I bit my tongue to hold back my true feelings about fate, justice, and fairness, not to mention how I felt about Melissa, her silliness and her utter lack of tact. But she wasn't the only one to have disregarded my failed conception attempts. I'd been so naïve, so Alice in Wonderland about what was really going on with us. But I was getting an education and facing reality. It was time to admit to myself that something was wrong and that I needed to seek some help.

I knew to be wary of self-diagnosis based on Internet medical advice and I was wary to cross-check any advice I found, but when I discovered an online fertility community, I knew I had found my people. The site had been designed in friendly shades of pink that were feminine without being cute. It seemed like a place I could find like-minded women in situations similar to ours, on the same mission as me. At the very least I hoped to find empathy, but what I really wanted was a secret elixir. I signed up and soon discovered enough tools and widgets to keep my inner nerd happy for hours. I could chart and graph almost every aspect of my reproductive cycle from temperature to cervical mucus and energy levels to symptoms. I could even compare my charts to those of other women,

presumably to see if I was "normal." I looked forward
to the scientific aspect of this and made plans to start
immediately. But first I headed to the discussion boards,
hoping to find someone else out there, a kindred spirit,
who was facing the same issues.

I was hungry for information and almost giddy with
the thought of finally having people to talk to who had
been in the trenches and were armed with facts and all
the solutions to my problems. I clicked through to the
discussion boards and was thrilled to find women from
my tribe. There were women over 30 (me), women
trying for a first baby (me), even women whose
husbands had undergone vasectomy reversals (me, me,
me!). Finally, I was among my own people. I signed up,
paid my membership fee, and dived into my research. I
sifted through the threads to see what issues were being
discussed and more importantly, what solutions were
working. Some women were taking supplements like
Black Cohosh and False Unicorn Root, some were trying
alternative therapies—acupuncture or yoga. A staggering
proportion was taking fertility drugs. I was curious to
find out what they'd been through to get to so drastic
a stage, but I needed to stay focused on my own
mission and so opted for the vasectomy reversal group
instead. I found a thread entitled "Trying after VR," which
I assumed stood for Vasectomy Reversal. I clicked open
the thread.

"DH and I are TTC 6 mo. Now 8dpo, no sign of AF,
all neg HPTs."

These women may have been my tribe, but they
certainly weren't speaking my language, or any language
I'd seen before. I studied the post and tried to decipher
the terminology as best I could. I figured out quickly that
TTC stood for "Trying to Conceive" and that DH had
something to do with the father. I ran the possibilities
through my mind and came up with Donor or Daddy

for the "D" and Husband for the "H," but the combinations didn't make any sense. I scanned a few more posts in the hope that someone had slipped and forgotten to use the code, but as far as I could tell, I was the only incompetent one using the site. Without some explanation, most of the posts were gobbledygook.

I Googled "Fertility Abbreviations" and found a site with a complete list of explanations. I returned to the discussion boards, feeling smug, as if I'd just learned the Fred Flintstone secret Masonic handshake, and translated the thread: "My *Darling Husband*" (Darling Husband— I would never have come up with that on my own) "and I have been *Trying To Conceive* for six months. Now eight *Days Past Ovulation*, no sign of *Aunt Flow*, all negative *Home Pregnancy Tests*." I went over it again to make sure I'd read it correctly and realized something was fishy. I knew that a normal reproductive cycle was approximately 28 days long, 14 days in the Follicular Phase, where the eggs grow and mature, then ovulation happens and an egg is released; then the next 14 days is the Luteal Phase, where the egg heads off down the Fallopian tube in the hopes of being fertilized and implanting in the uterus. Even with a short cycle, eight days after ovulation seemed too soon to be taking a Home Pregnancy Test and wigging out about a negative result. On the one hand, I could understand the anxiety of waiting to find out—I'd experienced that every month for the last six months—but now I knew better than to take a test early and risk the disappointment of a false-negative test. Obviously, this woman was a little fanatical. I left her thread and went in search of saner "friends."

Everybody seemed so knowledgeable about all the details of infertility and I soon learned the steps involved in IVF, the names of the most common fertility drugs, and the herbs and supplements most favored. I became fluent in the secret language of infertility, and learned the subtle but important difference between AF (Aunt Flow) and BFN (a Big Fat Negative pregnancy test). Aunt Flow was the pet name for a period, a sure sign that any chance of being pregnant that month was over; BFN, according to the boards, meant that things weren't looking good, but there still was hope.

Hope was the key word among the women on the boards. They seemed almost joyful to post tickers of their cycles so that when ovulation approached, other members could liberally scatter Baby Dust—the fertility equivalent of magic fairy dust—as a good-natured, if scientifically useless, aid to conception. Some had posted photos of their furbabies—the pets acting as baby substitutes until the real thing came along—and I was relieved to see that I wasn't the only woman whose cat had to tolerate being cradled and having raspberries blown on her belly. We were all hoping for the same outcome and wishing the best for one another. The consensus was that if one of us got out with a baby, it meant there was hope for the rest of us. Pretty soon, I was handing out advice to newcomers and madly sprinkling Baby Dust with my online friends, Baby Dreams, One Good Swimmer, and Hopefully Mama.

But after a few weeks of participating, I began to get a different sense of the groups. Along with the hope and encouragement, I noticed a trend of fanaticism. I had intimate details of my new friends' sex lives and knew the finite details of each woman's cycle. One woman had even posted an X-ray of her reproductive organs so we could all see her healthy fallopian tubes. I had to admit that I was fascinated by the image, not at all like the neat drawings in the books. Her uterus seemed to lean to one side and her tubes looked like jellyfish tentacles, so fine and delicate that they couldn't possibly have been up to the job of transporting eggs. At the end of each tube was a knobby clump of ovary, nothing like the delicate fan shown in textbooks. It was beautiful and monstrous at the same time.

I knew when strangers were planning to have sex (or do the BD—Baby Dance) and I knew exactly how many days they would be waiting to see if their efforts had been successful. Underneath the warm words and support, I sensed an air of desperation that rushed along, dragging everyone with it towards the center of the universe, a BFP— a Big Fat Positive pregnancy test.

When I'd graduated from single woman to married-woman-trying-to conceive, I'd felt proud and superior, but now I'd joined a different group, a kind of secret underground sisterhood. We'd signed up under pseudonyms (I'd borrowed my cat's name) so as not to reveal our true identities, and then shared every intimate detail of our personal and medical histories. I knew more about these women I'd never met than I did about my own friends. We were in a class of our own, not allowed to play with the other kids—the women with babies.

I decided to stick with my own kind in the online group, but I made a mental note to keep my distance and not get pulled into the insanity. I wanted to have a baby, very much so, but I didn't want it to rule my life. I had been lucky enough to find a wonderful man and we shared an interesting and sometimes exciting life together. We had things to talk about, places we wanted to visit, thoughts and opinions on subjects ranging from politics to theater to airline deals to good cheese. Trying to have a baby was just a part of who I was, and I could see that for many of the women online, it had consumed them and infiltrated every corner and crevice of their lives.

With every passing month, the posts I read disturbed me more. I was increasingly alarmed at the number of women taking Clomid and those undergoing multiple

IVFs. I had been wrong about it being a miracle cure, something that happened only as a very last resort. I was seeing thousands of women who had embarked on this journey of pills, and shots, miracle treatments and unbelievable lengths to have a baby of their own.

Finally I came across the following post:

IVF #3
4/15- BCP's
5/18- Start stims
5/30- Egg Retrieval- 36 retrieved, 24 fertilized!!
6/14- Embryo Transfer

I still didn't understand all the abbreviations, but I understood clearly 36 eggs retrieved and 24 fertilized. I was stunned. How did this woman get 36 eggs ready for retrieval? And of the 24 fertilized, how many were transferred to her uterus and what happened to the rest? I couldn't imagine the quantity of drugs she had to pump into her body to force it to perform such feats. And I couldn't imagine the state of desperation she must have been in to agree to do that.

Or could I?

After less than a year of trying, Jose and I were getting used to the monthly disappointment, which didn't make it any less disappointing. We'd set off on a journey, expecting to get pregnant and slowly discovering that it wasn't the simple, natural process we'd thought it would be. Jose had quit coffee and wine, stopped using his laptop, and avoided his bike because I'd read in a book that all these things could reduce his fertility. I'd taken advice from my new online friends and bought expensive supplements and a conception kit, designed to help get Jose's sperm closer to my cervix and ultimately my fertile eggs. I'd taken to sliding off the bed after sex and resting, upside-down, with my shoulders on the ground, hips on the bed, in the hopes of propelling Jose's slow-moving sperm along to their destination. None of this had worked for us, and I was already waiting, looking, searching, for the next big thing, the secret to our fertility success.

So, reading through the various posts, I could track the path of that woman's desperation. Even though each woman had her own personal timeline, the path still followed the same pattern of events. *We tried this and it didn't work, so now we're going to try something else. We tried the something else and that didn't work, so someone recommended adding this.* Over the course of time it was easy to see how someone could get to the point of forcing her body to produce three-dozen eggs.

I thought back to my friend Chris, who'd tried for so long to have a baby, and I realized that she had traveled this path and maybe even reached a similar point as this woman. I wished I had been more attuned to her plight, that I'd had more knowledge and been more supportive. But I hadn't been traveling in these circles then. I hadn't opened that door into infertility; it hadn't been on my radar screen then. But I was here now, standing on the edge of this vast new universe for the first time, seeing the possibilities and all the paths that I could take, all the decisions I might have to make. I didn't know what lay ahead for Jose and me, if we were weeks away from becoming pregnant, or months. All I knew was that it wasn't working and sooner or later, we were going to need some help. And I knew I didn't want to become so obsessed that I would force my body to perform inhuman tricks. The Internet was an invaluable source of information, but it could also be a dangerous path to self-diagnosis, based solely on the opinions of others. It was time to seek professional help. Not knowing where else to start, I made an appointment with my OB/GYN and one for Jose with his GP. Even if these trusted doctors couldn't help us, they could refer us to someone who could.

8
In Docs We Trust?

Year 2

Doctor Bennett filled the room with an overwhelming sense of trust. Although she'd been my official OB/GYN for several years, I'd never actually met her before, and had always seen the Nurse Practitioner for my annual exam. She breezed into the exam room wearing golden cornrows and a broad smile, shook my hand warmly and said, "Are you being treated for that goiter?"

My hand flew up to cover the unsightly swelling that spoiled an otherwise long, lean neck. My GP had poked at my swollen neck every time I saw her and had tested my thyroid and deemed that the results showed nothing unusual, so I'd simply learned to live with my fat neck.

"No," I said.

Doctor Bennett shook her head and immediately wrote me a referral to an endocrinologist; she had no doubt there was something very wrong with my thyroid and a specialist would get to the root of the problem. "It's important we get this fixed," she said. "The thyroid can affect fertility."

My eyes flew open at what she was suggesting, that

the reason I was not yet pregnant might have something to do with me, and not just Jose and his sperm count. It had been a year since Jose's surgery and although his sperm count was still low, his doctor saw no reason why I shouldn't be able to get pregnant. Now Doctor Bennett was suggesting a reason.

Before I could process the thought, the conversation turned to the fertility workup, which Doctor Bennett suggested I begin immediately. "We'll do an FSH test first—that's a simple blood test—and I'll also send you for an HSG. Unfortunately that's the most expensive and uncomfortable test, but it will eliminate the most likely cause first. If that's clear, we'll move to the next possibility."

For a moment I felt like Alice again, falling down, down, down the rabbit hole into a strange Wonderland, where people used made-up words like FSH and HSG—but the journey wasn't entirely unpleasant. Doctor Bennett was efficient and competent, but most of all compassionate. She'd know what to do to get me my baby.

Once home, I researched goiters, thyroids, FSH, and HSGs. I knew a bit about FSH, the hormone responsible for stimulating the egg follicles and inducing ovulation. The test was conducted on the second or third day of the cycle and used to make sure the body's hormone levels were normal. An FSH higher than 10 suggested that something was wrong with the ovulation process and so more hormone was needed in order to cause an egg to release. FSH increased with age as menopause approached, but since I was only 36, I didn't expect to find any problems.

Next I found a list of symptoms related to hypothyroidism and was shocked to see how many of them I had. Significant fatigue, constipation, low sex drive, weight gain, skin problems, loss of concentration, feeling cold. I'd experienced all of these, but had always chalked them up to some other explanation. I was tired all the time because I got up early, exercised hard and worked long hours; it made sense that I had the ability to fall asleep almost anywhere and at any time of day. I'd attributed my scaly skin to a reaction to some soap or detergent and had been experimenting with brands to find one that suited me better. A low sex drive had to be expected in someone who'd been trying unsuccessfully to conceive for well over a year.

There was one symptom on the list that almost made me laugh: loss of the outer edges of the eyebrows. It was such a strange indication and so specific. I hurried to the bathroom, switched on the lights around the mirror, and peered at my eyebrows. On the bridge of my nose I had fuzzy stray hairs that needed plucking again, and some stragglers below my brow bone that needed tidying up, but the outside edges were thin and clean, so thin and clean that my brows no longer lined up with the outside corners of my eyes: loss of the outer edge of the eyebrows. I went back to the book and stared at the list of symptoms, and my eyes fell square on the last symptom in the list: *infertility.* I felt the cells in my body shrivel as I realized I had a thyroid problem and that it could be preventing me from getting pregnant. The endocrinologist would know for sure and I was suddenly afraid of what this might mean for my future.

If I'd been worried about my visit to the endocrinologist, that fear was quickly superseded by my research into the HSG. The test, a hysterosalpingogram, involved injecting dye into the uterus and fallopian tubes so that x-rays could be taken to ensure there were no blockages or obstructions. Depending on which website I read, my pain expectations ranged from "mild discomfort" to "worse than the vaginal birth of twins."

One morning while out walking with a friend, I told

her that I was going for a test. Her face turned suddenly ashen. "I did that before I had my son. It was the most excruciating pain ever—worse than giving birth."

"Really?" I said, perhaps hoping she'd change her opinion.

She shook her head. "It was so bad I had to tell them to stop."

"Didn't they give you painkillers or something?"

"They told me to take a couple of Tylenol beforehand, but it didn't do any good."

I tried to convince myself that my friend just had a low tolerance for pain and that I would be fine, but it was with great trepidation that I scheduled the appointment for my own test.

On the morning of the test I took my Tylenol and Jose drove me to the medical center, even though it was just a few short blocks from my house. I tried to make light chitchat all the way to reassure him that I wasn't afraid, but I think he saw through my performance; he didn't joke back. He walked me to the radiology department and gave me a kiss, telling me he'd in the waiting room when I was done. I watched him go and then I followed the radiology tech into the exam room. I perched nervously on the edge of the table, surrounded by expensive machinery and monitors. The technician smiled and carefully explained very exactly what was going to happen. She was so kind and gentle that I felt reassured. "It can be pretty painful," she said, "but you lucked out getting Doctor Curtis. She's fast and gentle."

She showed me into an adjoining bathroom where a paper gown had been laid out for me. I closed and locked the door behind me and began to undress. I felt tired suddenly, drained of all my energy, even the nervous energy I'd had all morning. Stepping out into the exam room, dressed only in a thin paper robe, I felt as if I was stepping out into nothing. It reminded me of skydiving—something I hadn't done since I was 20 years old. I had trained for a day and then climbed aboard an old doorless Cessna and flew up to 3,000 feet. When it was my turn to jump, I quivered with anticipation. I edged to the open door and looked down at the ground 3,000 feet away. There was a whole lot of nothing between it and me. The only thing I knew for sure about the next few minutes of my life was that at some point I would hit the ground—preferably attached to an open parachute—and that no matter how afraid I was, eventually, it would be over.

This time, as I waited for Doctor Curtis to arrive, I couldn't see the ground. I was stepping out into a void with no visible edges. I was being tested for infertility because I hadn't been able to conceive. After this test, there'd be more tests, and more, until someone figured out why I couldn't have a baby. And then there'd be treatments and procedures, maybe even surgeries. And after all that, I still didn't know if I'd ever have a baby. I didn't know if I'd ever hit the ground.

The technician kept up a steady stream of chatter while she positioned me on the table and set up the equipment to take x-rays. She asked open-ended questions, clearly designed to keep me talking and keep my mind off the activity going on around me. While we waited for the doctor to arrive, she told me about the three young siblings she had recently adopted and showed me photos of their mischievous, lovable faces. I couldn't help but wonder if she'd been through this same procedure and discovered that she was unable to have children of her own. I realized that she was probably thinking similar thoughts about me, wondering what my story was. I had graduated to a different class of woman. I was no longer the excited newlywed trying to start a family. I had become this other being, an infertile woman, trying to crack the code that would allow me to have a baby.

Doctor Curtis was as efficient and gentle as advertised. She inserted a catheter into my cervix, explaining at every step what she was going to do, why she was going to do it, and how it was going to feel. Next she injected the dye and explained that the pain I would feel was cramping. I knew how to deal with cramps and took deep breaths and tried to stay relaxed. She moved quickly, rolling my hips to one side and then the other. I could feel the surge in pain as the dye ran into my fallopian tubes, but I kept my eyes shut and kept my mind on my baby, imagining how it would feel to hold a child of my own against my breast, and knowing that any pain now would be worth that feeling.

"Your left tube is closed," said the doctor. "With your permission, I want to increase the pressure and try to blow it open."

Without hesitation, I nodded that it would be okay and steeled myself for the pain. A sharp thought kept poking its way through the waves of cramping: *one tube is closed; my odds of getting pregnant have only been half; one chance every two months.* Punctuating those thoughts was the stark realization that there was something else wrong with me—first the goiter and now a blocked tube. I was not the perfect specimen of health I'd always believed. It was possible that I was to blame for the fact that I could not conceive, and I felt helpless and oddly duped.

And then the procedure was over. The doctor had opened up the tube and explained that it should stay that way for a while. "Having this test can actually increase your chances of getting pregnant, because the tubes are more open. Good luck," she said, as I shuffled back to the bathroom and began the process of cleaning the dye, the lubrication gel, and the spots of blood from around the tops of my legs.

One of my favorite board games has always been The Game of Life. I get great pleasure from tearing around the board, filling my red car with pink and blue pegs, making decisions about my future, and dealing with life's little ups and downs. The Fertility Game wasn't nearly as much fun. I was the pawn, waiting while someone else spun the wheel and decided on my next move. My role was to do as instructed, shuttling from one doctor to the next, taking tests as ordered—HSG, FSH—following a route without ever being shown the layout of the board. The doctors knew the game and held the power, while the patient followed along, waiting to see what happened next. I felt lost and vulnerable, unclear what lay ahead for me. All I could do was trust that the doctors knew the rules and would always do what was best for me.

"I'd go straight for IVF," Doctor Bagayan said. "You're probably going to end up there anyway." She was Jose's GP and, along with my fertility workup, we had decided to make an appointment with her to see if she had any suggestions as to how we could improve the quality of Jose's sperm. She had a pained look in her eye that made me think she was speaking not from scientific protocol, but from personal experience. I wanted to ask her if she had children, if she'd been through this experience, but it seemed wholly inappropriate. We asked if acupuncture and herbs might help, and if there were less invasive procedures than IVF, less drastic steps that might help us to conceive. "You can try," she said. "But why waste the time and money?" She handed us a card for a nearby fertility clinic and told us to go and see Doctor Hassan. "He's very good at what he does. I can recommend him highly."

We left the office with a sense of unease. This hadn't

been the visit we'd expected. Doctor Curtis had blown open my closed tube, I had an appointment set with the endocrinologist, and, as I hadn't received a call from my doctor, I assumed my FSH levels were normal. I was convinced that the main problem we had was getting Jose's sluggish sperm up to and into my egg. I had been picturing Jose taking sperm-boosting supplements for a few months, maybe finding some way to shoot them closer to my incoming egg. It seemed so obvious to me and yet Doctor Bagayan was adamant: IVF or nothing.

We got in the car. "She's an idiot," said Jose.

I was inclined to agree, but feeling charitable, I made excuses for her. "She's trained in western medicine; that's all she knows. She's clearly not knowledgeable enough in alternative therapies to be open to them."

"You're very kind," Jose said, somewhat begrudgingly.

In reality, I was clinging to the idea that there were other options open to us if we could find out what they were, but I couldn't get Doctor Bagayan's expression out of my mind. Maybe she was speaking from experience and maybe she'd tried other methods. Maybe she could clearly see the layout of the board game and was trying to save us the agony of taking the longer route to the same place.

We drove home, both feeling further away from our goal than before our appointment.

Over the summer, Jose changed jobs and his mother fell ill; both events gave us something to focus on besides trying to make a baby. I saw the endocrinologist, who diagnosed an enlarged thyroid and prescribed thyroid replacement medicine. This was the first time I had ever been diagnosed with a chronic condition and I threw myself into researching treatment and symptoms and trying to figure out if and how this might affect my fertility and if there was a way to treat my condition without having to resort to drugs. I already knew that thyroid conditions can very much affect fertility if gone untreated, but the endocrinologist saw no reason that my particular condition should prevent me from getting pregnant. I hated that I would have to take medication for the rest of my days, but as my energy increased, my skin problems cleared and the edges of my eyebrows began to grow back, I resigned myself to the fact that some conditions just had to be medicated. All this activity had pushed our fertility issues down the list of priorities. But as Thanksgiving approached and I still wasn't pregnant, I was forced to admit to myself that I'd been making excuses. It was time to go to the fertility doctor and reluctantly say, "I am infertile and I need help."

I was filled with apprehension as I approached the pink granite building that housed Doctor Hassan's office. It was an imposing, important-looking building, the kind of place where miracles of science happened behind closed doors. I had never expected to find myself at a fertility clinic, and I still wasn't certain this was the right place for me. The glossy brochure that the doctor's office had sent prior to our appointment had been filled with smiling baby faces and highlights of all the procedures available. The only one that seemed to apply to our situation was Inter-Uterine Insemination, a relatively simple procedure that involved injecting Jose's sperm directly into my uterus after I had ovulated—exactly the procedure I had envisioned at Doctor Bagayan's office. In any case, I knew that Doctor Hassan would have all the available knowledge on reproductive medicine laid out before him and he would be able to suggest the best options for us.

Inside the building, I had a distinct recollection of something I'd once seen on TV about a milk bottling plant. The factory in my memory was sparkling and pristine, with shiny milk bottles rattling down conveyor belts, shuttling off to other machines, to the happy clanking of glass against metal, where they were filled with fresh wholesome milk and capped with silver foil lids, and then shuttled off to crates for delivery. My image of the whole process was of a brisk, efficient operation, where a single speck of dirt could shut down the entire system. I had the same feeling when the elevator doors opened onto the second floor of the fertility clinic.

The milk bottles in this scene had been replaced by doctors, nurses and technicians, bustling along corridors and disappearing behind white doors with shiny chrome handles. Everybody seemed to know exactly where they were supposed to be and exactly what they were supposed to be doing, which left me feeling dazed and more lost than ever. I made my way into a large reception area and made myself known to the receptionist. She pulled out a packet of forms, asked for my insurance and credit cards and pointed me to a row of straight-backed upholstered chairs. I glanced around the room, taking in the gentle modern prints hung on the walls, and the soft, comforting colors of the furniture. I floated by a wall filled with pictures and cards thanking the doctors for the gift of a miracle. My eyes scanned over the blonde-haired blue-eyed babies until I found a dark-haired baby that could have been mine. My stomach lurched and I felt a surge of desire for a baby of my own. I wanted to see my baby's picture hanging on this wall, hanging on my wall at home, slotted into a photo holder in Jose's wallet, and framed, slap-bang in the middle of grandma's mantelpiece. It wasn't fair that I didn't have that yet and it wasn't fair that I had to be in a fertility clinic to make that dream a reality.

I was alarmed, but not surprised by the number of twins, triplets, and even quads among the laughing baby faces. I'd become aware of the number of double strollers I saw in my local park and being pushed around my neighborhood, and I knew of at least two sets of triplets who lived close-by. I'd also seen the media frenzy that surrounded miracle families like the McCaughey septuplets. Natural multiple births weren't very common and I knew that most of these babies were the result of fertility treatments. I'd always wanted to have twins, expected to really, because of my genes and my mother's needle test, but I didn't want to publicize my infertility and twins were now like a giant billboard saying, "I took fertility drugs! Look at me!" In the neighborhood where I lived, twins had almost become a status symbol, a way of showing that you could afford the very best treatment to overcome infertility.

Reproductive medicine is incredible technology, but like any science, must be respected. We have become an instant solution society. Got high blood pressure? Pop a pill. Need to lose 50 pounds? Pop a pill. Can't have a baby? Pop a pill. I felt very protective of my body and wasn't willing to subject it to just any prescribed treatment. I once had a friend who would go through bottles of pills for her constant headaches. If I got a headache, I wanted to know why. Was I tired, hungry, thirsty, stressed? Had I exercised too much, eaten something I'd reacted to, drank too much beer the night before? When something was wrong with me, I wanted to treat the cause, rather than the symptoms. And I felt the same way about my visit to Doctor Hassan. I wanted him to use his expertise to figure out *why* I couldn't get pregnant and find a solution to *that* particular problem. If our problem was Jose's sperm quality, how could we fix that problem? How could we make it stronger and healthier so that I could get pregnant?

Jose was late to the appointment. And in a bad mood. I could tell he was in his busy, get-things-done work mode. He had his take-no-prisoners expression on

his face. I didn't need this. I wanted him to be receptive
to the possibilities the doctor might present. I needed
him to keep his mind open, not have tunnel vision. The
truth was, I wanted him to be nice, so that the doctor
would like us and decide we deserved to have a baby
and would want to do everything he could to help us. It
was ridiculous to think a doctor wouldn't do that just
because he didn't like the look of us, but I still wanted
to come across as a nice kind of patient, someone who
wouldn't be difficult. I didn't want to be any trouble.

Before long, a short, bald-headed man swept through
the lobby and from the way the air seemed to part
around him, I knew this was the doctor. We were hustled
along in his wake and ushered into his corner office,
where he asked how he could help. We explained our
situation. He looked at the papers I handed him showing
Jose's sperm test results and evidence of my open tubes
and almost textbook-perfect cycle charts. He passed the
papers from one hand to the other, nodding to himself.
I slid my hand onto Jose's leg and underneath his hand.
I gave it a squeeze and was surprised when he didn't
squeeze back. I squeezed again, trying to elicit a loving
"we're-in-this-together" response, but Jose didn't react. I
could feel him pulling further away and I began to panic.
I didn't want to be here alone.

"IVF is the only way," said the doctor, looking up
finally and making eye contact with Jose, but not
with me.

I felt as if I was no longer in the room with them, as
if they were having this discussion about my future
without me. I sat in stunned silence, trying to process
what the doctor was saying. Had he considered all the
other options? What about the Inter-Uterine Insemination
we'd seen in the brochure? It seemed as if that would be
more logical, placing Jose's sperm right up close to my
approaching egg. After all it was Jose's sperm that was

the issue; I was being treated for my thyroid condition and both fallopian tubes were in working order, so why did I need to undergo a procedure like IVF? It didn't make sense. I found my voice and put my question to the doctor, trying to keep the shock from showing in my voice. He shook his head again. "IVF is the only way," he repeated. He picked up the phone and began dictating our case to someone or something on the other end of the line.

His prognosis seemed so final, so black-and-white, on-or-off, get pregnant naturally or by IVF. My world didn't work that way. There was always grey in between. In my experience, people were never right or wrong, there was almost always something of value, even in an opinion I didn't share. I could usually understand someone's point of view, even if I didn't agree. There was always a part of the wrong that was right and some of the right that was wrong. Over my lifetime, I'd come to count on the grey areas as places where solutions could be found, where opinions and possibilities could be combined to find some kind of common ground. As human reproduction was such an imprecise science, based on chance and the right combination of hormones, timing, and environment, it was rife with grey areas. I had, naturally, expected grey areas in reproductive medicine, too. I'd expected that one technique might work for one person but not for another. I'd been counting on the grey to find the least intrusive solution for us, but Doctor Hassan was offering a black-and-white, one-size-fits-all solution.

The problem was, it didn't fit me.

As the doctor led us from his office, I glanced at Jose. I'd expected him to look sad or shocked, but his expression was almost blank. I could tell he didn't like Doctor Hassan; I just couldn't tell exactly why.

Without further explanation, the doctor led us to an

office where a young woman greeted us with a warm smile. "Heather will explain the procedure to you," said the doctor, and he left. As the door closed behind him, I realized he was going back to his office to meet the next patient and that we, just like those shiny milk bottles, had been passed to the next stage of the production line.

Heather smiled and pushed a paper calendar in front of us. "This is how it works," she said. Her words ran over my head as I tried to keep up, but all the while thinking, "*Who said we were going to do this?*" Was it just assumed that because Doctor Hassan had deemed this our only solution that we would go along without question? I sat there and listened while Heather outlined when I'd be put on birth control pills to regulate my cycle, and when I'd begin taking Lupron, a medication designed to suppress ovulation and put my body into a state similar to menopause. I could feel the fury building up inside me at the gall these people had for assuming I would just throw myself at their mercy and subject my body to all these drugs and procedures. But I didn't say a word, because a little voice, somewhere in the back of my head kept saying, *What if this is the only way? Wouldn't it be worth it to have a baby of your own? You want to have a baby, don't you?* I did. I really did. And so I sat there, mute, like a good obedient patient while Heather explained how I'd administer my shots, when to start the shots of Follicle Stimulating Hormone and when I'd need to start taking Medrol, Heparin, Baby Aspirin, and hCG. Baby Aspirin was the only medication I'd ever heard of before, but I had no idea why I would need to take it and Heather didn't take the time to explain.

"We want you to produce a good selection of eggs," said Heather, "as many as fifteen, so we monitor all this very carefully and adjust the dose as needed."

Fifteen eggs? I thought about the triplets and twins whose pictures graced the lobby walls and I thought back to the woman online who'd been so excited about the 36 eggs that had been retrieved. I thought about the McCaughey septuplets, and I thought, *this is wrong. This isn't what our bodies are supposed to do.* This wasn't what I *wanted* to do either, but still the little voice kept squawking in my head, *Only way, only way, what if it's the only way?*

"How many we implant depends on the patient," said Heather, "but it can be anywhere from two to seven, depending on your age, medical history and also your risk aversion."

"What do you mean by *risk aversion?*" Jose asked. He'd been so quiet I'd almost forgotten he was there.

"It's important to discuss this with the doctor first," said Heather. "He will need to know if you're prepared to deal with multiple births." I'd spent most of my life anticipating having twins; I was more than prepared for that, but not for triplets or quads, and certainly not for septuplets. I didn't want *my* family turned into a media circus.

"There is an option for selective fetal reduction," said Heather, "but some people, because of their religious beliefs or whatever, aren't willing to do this. In this case, the doctor would recommend transferring fewer embryos. Obviously, the more embryos that can be transferred, the higher the success rate."

I didn't have any religious or political objection to a woman's right to choose to have a child—or four children—or not, but there was something fundamentally unethical about *deliberately* creating new life only to destroy it. I wondered if Heather agreed.

"After two weeks," said Heather, "we'll do a pregnancy test, which we hope will be positive." She grinned. "We'll keep you on progesterone for three months just to make sure your body holds the pregnancy and once you're out of your first trimester, you'll be released into regular OB care."

So even if I was able to get pregnant by this method, I still wouldn't be properly pregnant, not really. My body would continue to fight against my fetus and against the things it had been forced to do and I'd need to take more drugs to keep my body in line until it finally gave in and accepted the pregnancy.

"What about the side effects?" I asked. I knew I couldn't fell her with any of my moral arguments, she had been inculcated already, but maybe I could get her on scientific grounds. I knew in my gut this was all wrong and I wanted her to see it, too.

"What about the long-term side effects on the mother, or on the baby?" I asked her.

I must have found the chink in the armor, because Heather looked uncomfortable suddenly and her sweet smile fell for just a moment. She mumbled something about long-term studies and side effects, but it was not clear if long-term studies had shown no side effects, or if there had been no long-term studies showing side effects.

I felt utterly dazed. I knew I was in the room, hearing this list of things that was going to be done to me, but it didn't seem real. I'd never had any medical procedures except having a fractured ankle put in a cast. I'd had no need for medications other than antibiotics and my newly prescribed thyroid medication. I'd never had the need for a foreign object to be placed inside my body, or for any part of my body (except a couple of teeth) to be removed. But here I was being told that all these things would happen to me if I went through with IVF.

When Heather was done, she led us from her office, down the stairs, along the production line to the next procedure. I felt defeated, exhausted from processing all this information and from flipping back and forth between my feelings of horror and my overriding desire to have a baby. Jose walked beside me. As our arms touched I felt the static bristle of negative energy. He was furious, but was holding it all in. For that I was thankful. I didn't want a scene, just in case we decided to come back, just in case this *was* the only way.

Our last stop, the silver foil lid on our proverbial milk bottle, was Alma. She wore a sharp suit and a well-practiced smile, and was responsible for laying out the costs of an IVF procedure: $10,425 for one cycle, plus $3,000-$6,000 for medications. My mind began to spin wondering where we'd get that kind of money. I added up the credit left on each of our cards, threw in our savings, and figured we'd find a way to make the payment.

Alma whipped over the form and on the back, sketched out their other plans. She explained that by paying up front, we could save ourselves some money in the event of needing to do a second cycle of treatment, if the first one didn't work. Or, we could commit to three cycles and effectively get three go-arounds for the price of two.

"Oh, you're having a sale," said Jose. His sarcasm was lost on Alma, but I wanted to high-five him. What she was saying, to my ears, was that if we believed in the miracle, we should pay for just one cycle; if we had any misgivings, we should cut our losses and pay for three upfront. It was like dealing with a low-rent used car dealership, the flashy salesmen assuring us we couldn't live without his product, Heather explaining all the bells and whistles, and finally the closer, Alma, rubbing her hands together and saying, "Boy, do I have a deal for you."

I heard the little voice in my head that had kept saying, "What if it's the only way," begin to fade until it was little more than a low whistle somewhere in the fog of my mind.

Once home, I sat in the corner of the couch and cried—not giant sobs, but quiet, reassuring tears. I felt violated by these people, and right when I'd been most vulnerable. But I was safe now, and I'd never have to go back there again. Jose and I walked to the beach to talk it over. We discussed the whole experience, from Doctor Hassan's God-like attitude to Alma's Buy-2-Get-1-Free deal. We talked about the possibility of having multiple embryos implanted and having to make the decision to cull the ones we didn't want. There wouldn't be any we didn't want, but giving birth to four babies wouldn't be good for any of us. It would be a terrible decision to have to make. For three miles, to the end of Torrance Beach and back, we listed reason after reason why we couldn't go through with IVF.

"And where do we stop?" I asked. "If it doesn't work after three cycles, what then? At what point do we say, 'It's not meant to be for me to give birth,' and move on to another plan?"

Jose didn't know and neither did I.

"What if something's wrong with the kid?" he said, his voice quieter than ever. "What if he develops some terrible illness? I'd always be wondering if it was the drugs or the procedure. I wouldn't be able to live with myself if that happened."

For a week or so my emotions careened between sorrow, indignation, fury, and repulsion. I argued that other women went through this procedure and had perfectly healthy babies all the time. I looked for reports stating the health dangers of fertility drugs, but could come up with no concrete evidence. Regardless, the feeling in my gut told me that IVF wasn't something I was willing to do.

Finally, my logical mind regained control and I realized that what the doctor had told us didn't make any sense. Jose's sperm count was indisputably low, but the tests I'd taken so far indicated no prohibitive issues with me. My cycle was as regular as clockwork, my hormone levels were all normal, my HSG had opened my tubes, and I had no previous history of any ailments that could be inhibiting my fertility. It seemed that Jose and I had all the raw materials for making a baby; they just needed to be put together. Suddenly, the doctor's no hope prognosis made no sense. With no further testing, he had labeled us hopelessly infertile and shuttled us into an expensive, emotionally and possibly physically dangerous scientific option. And I had almost bought it. For a short while it had looked like something solid for me to grasp onto.

Later that week, when I saw a quarter-page ad for the clinic in the local newspaper, any lingering faith I might have had in Doctor Hassan was completely erased. His clinic was hosting an open house for people interested in learning more about Assisted Reproductive Technology. The picture showed the doctor surrounded by hordes of his success stories. In the top corner was a large splash announcing that there would be a raffle at the party.

The grand prize was a free IVF Cycle.

9
Crazy Train: Ticket for Two
Year 3

Ovulation time was less than a week away when Jose got sick. He started with his usual once-a-year cold—the Man Flu, as my brother referred to it—a sniffle, a headache and some general moaning and requests for sympathy. Before long, though, this bout accelerated into a full-blown case of the genuine flu. Jose limped back to bed and I hurried after him, ministering care in the form of hot drinks, homemade soups, and the hot lemon powders—the only kind of cold medicine I would take—that I had my mum bring over from England. I tiptoed around the house so he could rest, and whenever I heard him wake up, I scurried in. When he said he wanted something sweet, I rushed out and came back with chocolate milk, *dulce de leche* ice cream, and two varieties of cookies. When he complained that his mother would never have left him alone, I didn't flinch. I massaged his forehead and made sympathetic mommy noises. I changed his sweaty sheets, ran out for boxes of Kleenex, and didn't complain when his coughing woke me up in the night. All in all, I played the perfect nurse.

But after three days, I'd had it.

His flu had passed and he was up and out of bed, but his body was sore from the days spent horizontal and he whined at every little twinge. He shuffled around the house, stooped over and groaning like a miserable old man. I suggested he take a hot bath to ease his sore muscles. "I hate sitting in my own dirty water," he grumbled. I suggested a short gentle walk, just to get him some fresh air and to get his circulation going again. "I don't have the energy for a walk," he said. We were just a day or two from ovulation; if he didn't pull it together, we were going to miss our opportunity to conceive. But he was so miserable and so unattractive, I didn't want to have sex with him anyway.

I was furious with Jose. How could he choose a time like this to get sick? And he wasn't even sick anymore, just recovering from sickness and I was sick of him being sick and sick of him recovering from being sick. Why couldn't he just get better?

"And you want to be a mother?" said a snarky little voice in the back of my head. I put my tail between my legs and went for a walk by myself.

Maybe I wasn't meant to be a mother. Not every woman is. Women became mothers for all kinds of reasons not related to mothering or nurturing. Women had babies to trap men, to please their own mothers, or because society and peer pressure cajoled them into it. I'd even heard of a woman with a hereditary disease who kept producing deaf children for the welfare money; she certainly wasn't meant to be a mother. I had friends who had been reluctant mothers. One had been leaned on by her husband, became pregnant on the first month off the Pill and had taken several years to really come to terms with her new role and bloom as an excellent mother. Another friend had vowed never to have children, suddenly became pregnant and, while she was a responsible mother, still resented the course her life had taken. Women became mothers by accident every day, either because they couldn't afford birth control, or it didn't work, or they just plain thought that getting knocked up could never happen to them. Some women chose to be mothers and then spent the rest of their lives full of regrets, wondering what might have been if they'd chosen another path.

And some women chose *not* to become mothers for just as broad a range of reasons. When I looked at my own circle of friends, it included strong, intelligent, and nurturing women who had chosen to forego motherhood. Karen had health concerns and didn't feel she could give the energy a child would need; Tammy had a history of addiction and abuse in her family and wasn't prepared to risk passing that legacy on to a child; Liz and her husband had decided that a family of two was all they needed to be complete. I had friends who were single, or in a relationship with someone who didn't want children, and had decided that they weren't prepared to make the journey into motherhood alone. These women were some of my dearest friends and I didn't think any less of them for their decisions; in fact I respected them more for their courage. I had once subscribed to the school of thought that choosing to be childless was selfish, but I had come to realize that deciding *not* to bring a child into a difficult situation was brave and selfless. Society still looked askance at childless women and wearing that banner proudly took an act of courage.

The Universe was offering me a chance to choose my path and decide the course of my own future. I wasn't going to fall into motherhood by accident and it didn't look as if it was going to come easily to me. If I wanted it, I was going to have to work for it. So, was it what I really wanted? Given the choice, would I choose to devote the rest of my life to another human being? Was I prepared to sacrifice things that were important to me, quiet time alone with my thoughts, the freedom to travel on a whim, a good night's sleep? Did I have the tenderness to nurse a sick child, the patience to handle tantrums, the tolerance to deal with someone else mucking up my plans?

With one bout of the flu, Jose had tested all these traits in me and I hadn't exactly risen to the occasion. But wouldn't I be different with a child? Wouldn't the natural instinct to be a mother kick in and take over? My own mother had admitted to a weak stomach for sickness, a short fuse of patience, and an affinity for peace and quiet, but she'd been an excellent mother— the best around, as far as I could tell. If she'd been a good mother, I could be, too.

I thought about having a child with Jose—Little Valentino or Sophia—a brand-new human being, a little bit of me and a little bit of him. I imagined feeling the skin of somebody who had been created from a part of me, wondering what it would feel like to touch an extension of myself. I imagined time spent with my child, reading my favorite stories and his favorite stories, explaining words and answering questions. I thought about taking my children out into the amazing world in which we live and showing them everything, taking them places, spending time with people from all walks of life, raising open-minded, tolerant, good people to send out into the world. I imagined my later years, white hair cut short or twisted into a loose knot, out in my garden, pruning my roses, discussing the state of the world with my grown children. I pictured intimate conversations with my daughters and I imagined holding my first grandchild for the first time. I could even picture my last days, peaceful days, at home in my own bed, surrounded by my wonderful family, preparing to say good-bye—and to rejoin Jose. I had a strong vision of what life would be like with children born of my own blood; it would be worth every single runny nose, temper tantrum, and sleepless night.

But how was I ever going to get my family if Jose and I never had sex? And even if we did manage to have unstrained, worry-free, flu-less sex, it didn't look as if I was going to get pregnant without some kind of help. Wild horses couldn't have dragged me back to Doctor Hassan and his baby factory, and the whole experience had turned me off western medicine.

Jose and I needed to regroup. We needed to figure out for ourselves how to make this work. We needed to be methodical and stay in control. I'd seen the crazy train other women had boarded and I wasn't about to buy a one-way ticket to insanity. Jose was the obvious problem—he was the one with the reversed vasectomy and the low sperm count—so it made sense to fix his issues first before turning the microscope on me. We needed real help for Jose, natural help to improve his sperm quality. The problem was, we had no idea where to turn next.

My friend Cassie was preparing to start trying for a baby, and provided an alternative solution.

"My acupuncturist told me that when I'm ready, she can help me get pregnant, like that!" she said, and snapped her fingers. My eyes flew open. I'd read books and web posts that touted acupuncture and traditional Chinese medicine as tried and true ways to improve fertility, but here was testimony from someone I knew. I'd known other people who'd cured ailments, or quit smoking using acupuncture—my Auntie Jean had sworn by it when she'd had back problems—so I knew there was something to it, but the person who'd made a true believer out of me had been my friend's dad Jim.

Jim had been diagnosed with cancer several years

before and had shunned western medicine in favor of more holistic methods. He and his wife, Anne, had become involved with an organization that explored the emotion-heart connection for curing illness. They had also adopted some of the more convenient principles of Christian Science and made frequent pilgrimages to San Francisco's Chinatown to visit a practitioner of traditional Chinese medicine. I had watched Anne measure strange looking dried herbs into a brown Chinese cooking pot and boil them for hours until the pungent odor of rotting leaves and stewing berries filled the entire house. The bookshelves of their little house in a small coastal senior community was filled with fascinating books about the mind-body connection and the power of self-healing. Their dedication to their beliefs and practices was fascinating to watch. Their whole lives revolved around healing Jim and keeping him alive. And it worked. When Jim's cancer was first diagnosed, he had been given six months to live. Ten years later, he was still going, still astounding his doctors, still keeping his cancer at bay. Jim and Anne had an aura of power about them and a belief that anything was possible. The air flowed gently around them somehow and I enjoyed being in their presence. They had beaten the odds and conquered cancer and they'd made me a believer in the power of the mind and the abilities of nontraditional healing.

But I didn't know if Jose would buy into it. He seemed open to nontraditional treatments—his former GP was an osteopath—but I wanted to tread carefully around the subject of his sperm quality and its treatment. I didn't want to point the finger of blame and say, "You're the problem; you need to be the solution." So I took a surreptitious tack.

"So, I was talking to Cassie," I said to Jose later that evening, "and she was telling me about her acupuncturist."

He looked up from the sperm-enhancing grilled salmon and steamed broccoli I now cooked for him as often as I could get away with it. "Oh?" he said, looking interested.

"I was thinking she might be able to help you with your shoulder."

Jose pressed his thumb against the old bike accident injury that had been giving him trouble lately and seemed to consider the idea. "Did you get her number?" he asked.

I nodded and handed him the scrap of paper on which Cassie had jotted a name and phone number. "What do you think?" I asked.

He cocked his head to one side. "I wonder if she could give me something to give the boys a boost, too," he said.

I widened my eyes as if the thought had never even occurred to me. "Well, she did seem to think that she could help get Cassie pregnant, like that." I snapped my fingers.

The next day, Jose made an appointment with Laura and by the end of the week he arrived home with a plain white bottle of pills and a list of supplements. There was no sign of the twigs and leaves and dried berries that I'd seen in Jim and Anne's kitchen. Instead, the bottle contained neat clear capsules filled with a green-brown powder, a concentrated form of an herbal tea—ancient medicine in a 21st century casing. Jose told me that when Laura had stuck the needles in his shoulder, he had experienced a shift in his body as if everything was moving across the table towards the needles. He claimed he had felt better almost immediately and was convinced that he'd soon be cured.

"Did you mention we were trying to get pregnant, too?" I asked eagerly.

"She said she could get you pregnant *like that*," he

said. He snapped his fingers and winked. "Which means there's going to have to be hot and cold running sex around here."

I forced a game smile and a poor excuse for a laugh. He was right; if we were going to do this "the old-fashioned way," there was going to have to be actual sex—well timed, fruitful, and preferably enthusiastic sex, at that.

On the surface, it sounded like an excuse for lots of early nights, leisurely weekend mornings in bed, and the occasional afternoon delight, but in reality, it was a chore. In the beginning, making love for babies had been exciting. We'd looked for any excuse to get Jose's sperm and my eggs together, but now, after two years of trying, the thrill was gone. All my tracking of temperature, cervical mucus, and LH surges had resulted in an accurate prediction of my most fertile window, a period of about three days. As the months passed and we forced ourselves to have sex as much as possible within that time frame, we felt less and less like making love at other times. Lately, our sex lives had been reduced to three reluctant rendezvous a month, in as many days. Jose didn't see my charts and graphs, but he could count and knew in advance when my Hot Zone was approaching. Even if he hadn't figured it out for himself, my sudden interest in him would have given it away. As the time approached, he took on the demeanor of a condemned man, shuffling into the bedroom to pay his penance for marrying me. I tried not be obvious, tried to pretend that my sudden interest in him was due to pheromones and not estrogen, but he always saw right through me. He would look resigned and I'd try my best to seduce him, but in the end, we'd go through the motions, both of us hoping it wouldn't take long, so we could be done with it, go to sleep, and forget that we'd have to do it all again the next night.

Sometimes, though, our minds got in the way of our bodies, and the harder we tried, the less likely it was that our endeavors would get the desired results. Those nights were the worst. Jose would be remorseful and I'd try to convince him that it was okay, that it didn't matter, that we'd try again the next day, but when we turned out the lights I would lay awake, calculating how many hours we had left before I'd pass my peak fertility and trying not to think about having to wait another month before we could try again. It was so frustrating. I felt as if we were running out of time and every month when I wasn't pregnant, I felt more and more as if it might never work. If it didn't work this time, why *should* it work next time?

I got the feeling I wasn't the only one who felt this way. Friends who knew we were trying and who had been so supportive in the early days no longer asked what was going on with us. And when someone did ask, the question seemed to jolt me back to reality and force me to acknowledge the fact that what we were going through just wasn't normal. The longer it went on, the more frustrated I became, but I knew I couldn't voice my disappointment to Jose. Adding additional pressure wasn't go to help him relax and get me what I needed, so I'd lay in the dark and let the tears of frustration roll down my cheeks and into my ears, and I'd try not to let him know I was crying.

When Jose's shoulder had stopped hurting and Laura had turned her focus to improving the quality of his sperm, Jose suggested that it might be prudent for me to see her too, just to make sure I was in tip-top condition. "Not that you need it, but it might help you relax about this whole thing."

I was trying to relax, trying to just let everything be, but when each month came around I became more determined to be ready, to time our sex just perfectly, and carry myself around as if wrapped in cotton, "just in case." I knew that relaxation was vital for conception, but getting pregnant was all I could think about and it was impossible to push from my mind the thought that it was taking so long, that the environment had to be perfect, and that our window of opportunity each month was really just a matter of hours.

And underneath all that was the beginning of an idea that maybe there was something wrong with me. I broached the subject with Jose on a couple of occasions, framing my concern as "what-if" rather than "I think maybe." His reaction was to dismiss me. "You're young," he said. "There's nothing wrong with you." He seemed as if he didn't want to hear of such a thing. Maybe he'd created a fantasy for himself that I was perfect, at least for him, and he didn't want to acknowledge any shortcomings on my part. Or maybe he just couldn't face the idea of me never having children; maybe he wanted to carry the blame for that on his own shoulders, or maybe he was just denying the possibility.

I also wanted to believe there was nothing wrong with me, because if I turned out to be the problem, everything he'd been through would be for nothing. I made an appointment with Laura determined to make sure I was in perfect health.

Laura was the furthest thing from the image I'd created of a wizened Chinese woman mixing potions in the dingy back room of a cramped office. She was pure West Los Angeles, with sharp funky outfits and fabulous shoes, thin body, neat hair, and virtually no makeup. Her office was hung with diplomas and Chinese scrolls, and decorated with Buddha statues and candles. I felt comfortable with her immediately. She asked questions I'd never been asked before. Did I get cold feet? Was I thirsty often? Then she asked me to stick out my tongue while she examined it, nodded and told me I was dehydrated, needed to cut out caffeine, and drink more water. Then she took my wrists and felt my pulse. She closed her eyes and appeared to be listening. She shifted her fingers slightly to a deeper point and listened again. "We need to strengthen your blood," she said, "but everything else feels good." I lay down on the table in her treatment room and waited while she stuck twenty or so needles at various points in my body. I'd expected it to hurt, but all I felt was the tiniest prickle. She turned down the lights and left me to relax. Within minutes I was fast asleep.

For the next few months, Jose and I made weekly, sometimes twice-weekly pilgrimages to Santa Monica to see Laura. She always asked questions about how we were, not just physically, but emotionally. She was empathetic and understood how difficult it could be trying to get pregnant. She seemed to genuinely want us to have a baby. Sure, she was running a business, but I felt as though she cared about our welfare. She firmly believed that she would soon see me pushing a stroller into her office. I could see the image clearly, too. All we had to do was to stay calm, take our herbs, take care of our bodies, and it would be only a matter of time. I could feel myself begin to let go of the anxiety of trying to have a baby and I felt as if my body was in safe hands, being healed and cared for, not filled with drugs and forced down a production line. I looked forward to my visits to Laura, to spending an hour in a peaceful nurturing environment, taking care of myself and preparing my body for motherhood.

Laura recommended yoga to further help relieve some of the stress, so I found a local Restorative Yoga class, signed up and, two hours later, floated home to Jose, relaxed and restored. I loved my yoga teachers and when I pulled each of them aside and explained I was trying to have a baby, they hugged me, showed me some poses, and added some to every class I took. "This pose creates a well in the abdomen," Kim would say, in her gentle lulling voice. "It pulls positive energy into the reproductive organs," she'd explain, and give me an encouraging smile. We always set an intention at the beginning of the class and I would sit cross-legged, my hands in prayer position at my heart center, and explain to the Universe that I was creating a nurturing environment into which it could send me a baby. A few months later, when Kim's belly began to push out the top of her yoga pants, I suppressed the whiny voice in my head that said, "That's not fair; it was supposed to be my turn." I breathed through the twisted knot that tweaked in my stomach and I wished her well, feeling certain that the Universe had simply missed its target and that my baby would be coming soon. The people into whose care I had placed myself shored up that confidence with gentle love and caring. We were all in this together, all trying to make a peaceful safe place for a baby to come.

The New Year came. It had been two-and-a-half years since Jose's surgery and three months since we'd begun seeing Laura. We went back to the urologist to check Jose's sperm, and got excellent news: the count had increased from two to nine million sperm per millimeter. It was still low, compared to the average figure of 20 million, but the big change had come in the sperm morphology. The slow-moving, misshapen specimens we'd seen before were now strong, fast-moving, and perfectly shaped. Laura had performed nothing less than a miracle. Jose and I beamed at one another; we had found the secret to our fertility success. Jose shared our secret with the urologist. "Keep it up then," the doctor said. "With these numbers, there's no reason why this shouldn't work."

Exactly, I thought.

There was a silent pause in the room and then the two men turned and looked at me. It took a second for the doctor's words to sink in and then the realization hit me: Jose was no longer the problem, which meant that now *I* was the reason we couldn't conceive. I began to panic. How could this be? My tests had all been okay, my thyroid was under control, there couldn't be anything else wrong with me. I felt the ground begin to waver underneath me as I tried to make sense of this. After all we'd been through with Jose, surely there couldn't be something wrong with me. But I knew right then that there was. I'd known when Doctor Curtis had told me that my tube was closed; I'd known when Doctor Bennett had first mentioned my goiter; and I'd known when, two-and-a-half years ago, Doctor Abrams had recommended a fertility workup before Jose committed to the surgery, and I had blown him off. I hadn't been in denial; I had been lying to myself. The difference was subtle. I hadn't been *unable* to admit I had a problem; I had flat refused to acknowledge my gut instinct, because admitting that there was something wrong meant admitting I was imperfect, and if Mother Nature had made me incapable of conceiving, then maybe I wasn't worthy of being a mother.

The urologist jotted down the name of another fertility doctor. "His bedside manner leaves something to be desired," he said, "but he's one of the best. He's also very conservative and will start with the least invasive possibility first." I took the paper and nodded, silent. After our first experience with fertility doctors, there was no way I was going to another. But I had to do something. I had a problem and I needed to fix it, but first I had to figure out *why* I couldn't conceive. I had to find the source of the problem and fix that. I clicked into mission mode.

I made a list of all the questions that had passed through my mind in the past two-and-a-half years, and all the theories I'd entertained and then dismissed. Why was my tube closed? Was it damaged? Was it twisted? Had it dried out and shriveled up like a dehydrated worm? And if so, why? And now that it was open, could it close again? What about my thyroid? Was I taking enough medication? Too much? Was my thyroid affecting something else that my endocrinologist hadn't thought of? What else could be wrong with me? Was I aging prematurely? Were the grey pubic hairs I'd discovered (when the hair on my head was still dark brown) a sign that my reproductive system was aging faster than the rest of me? Had something happened to me recently that had caused me to be unable to reproduce? Or had I been infertile all along? After all, I'd never been pregnant before.

I tried to think of every possibility, every permutation and combination of problems and causes. What if Jose and I weren't compatible reproductively? Maybe something in my chemistry was creating a hostile environment for Jose's sperm and preventing me from getting pregnant. Could it be fixed by diet? Was the lubricant we used damaging his sperm? Was I exercising too much and triggering some deep-seated instinct of the body to avoid reproduction in the face of hardship— migration, famine, or mammoth attack?

I thought about my environment and wondered if living in northern Europe in the late '80s had left me exposed to nuclear fallout from Chernobyl. I found fallout maps online and tried to remember if I'd visited any of the countries in the most exposed zones, or eaten foods grown there. Or maybe now I spent too much time in the proximity of computers and other radiating equipment. Perhaps the electrical fields were disrupting the messages from my brain to my ovaries, telling them not to send down an egg. The more I thought about it, the more harebrained my theories became and the more radical my list of solutions.

Armed with ideas and questions, I began my quest. I wiped the slate clean of all my old doctors and started again with a new set of opinions. I saw a new GP, a new OB/GYN, and the Reiki Master recommended by Laura. I expressed my theories to each and each suggested a new list of tests. I rolled up my sleeve and gave tube after tube of blood, had ultrasounds, x-rays, whatever they told me to do. I read books relating to all my possible theories and scoured the Internet for any grain of new information. I consumed information voraciously and went to work as an amateur medical sleuth, determined to solve the conundrum and expose the culprit. I tried every trick suggested and every product that looked even remotely effective.

What I needed was an advocate. I wanted someone who would look at me, look at my lifestyle, my diet, my medical history; someone who would study my test results, consider my thyroid, my age, my body's environment, and Chernobyl; someone who could step back and look at the big picture, see that the knee bone was connected to the thighbone, and figure out that my infertility was a result of X and Y, and could be fixed by Z. But no such person existed and it was up to me to be my own advocate, so I doubled up on my weekly acupuncture appointments and went to each one armed with a list of questions and hypotheses as to why I couldn't get pregnant. Laura listened and made suggestions. At one point she offered to connect me with friends of hers who had recently adopted a baby from Guatemala. I didn't consider that she might be giving up on me as a lost cause or that she might be observing the early symptoms of insanity in me; I just thought she was being helpful and offering options, and when I politely declined her offer, she recommended more tests and gave me more referrals to more doctors. It was what I wanted. I ran from appointment to appointment, giving samples of my blood, urine, and saliva. In the process I got parking tickets, a crumpled bumper, and a summons to traffic court for an overlooked registration renewal. I took time off work, time off from friends, and lots of time away from Jose. My only focus was figuring out what the hell was wrong with me and nothing was going to stand in my way.

I was desperate. Everywhere I went I got a clean bill of health. There appeared to be nothing physically wrong with me, so maybe my problem was spiritual. I set off to find the key that would unlock whatever forces were preventing me from conceiving. I meditated and went to yoga classes, I bought a fertility talisman and a large red penis-shaped candle, I searched the shops of Olvera Street, one of L.A.'s oldest districts, until I found a Catholic Saint candle depicting The Infant of Prague, said to aid fertility. I set up an altar in the bedroom, with the candle, an ancient mother figurine, and two tiny pairs of baby socks. I rallied my friends for their help and one brought me a fertility lobster. It was a dog toy really, in the shape of a lobster, but she'd been unable to find anything with any proven merit and it was no less valuable than any of the other talismans I'd tried and certainly no worse than the faith healer we had driven to see. He had shuttled us onto various couches around his house, laid his hands on and taken our money. Perhaps it wasn't his faith that was lacking, but ours. We were growing weary of wandering around in the dark, desperately searching without a map for a miracle we weren't even sure existed.

Finally, one afternoon, as I was leaving my third doctor's appointment of the day, I cracked. I had spent an hour talking to my GP while she had scratched her head and pulled books from the shelves trying to think of every possibility for why I wasn't pregnant. I appreciated her tenacity, but I was exhausted. Across the hallway, in the lab, I held out my arm while the lab tech took eight separate vials of blood. I watched as my deep red blood, rich from healthy foods and prenatal vitamins, pumped out into one vial after another. I could feel the life force draining from me with every thump of my heart, the last of my resolve seeping away into a glass tube. I didn't even know what most of the tests were for. I had just nodded to whatever the doctor said and held out my arm as instructed.

I took the elevator down the ten stories of the medical building and trudged out into the street. I stepped out into the crosswalk on Wilshire Boulevard, hoping the traffic would stop for me and not really caring whether it did or it didn't. Just as I reached the other side, my bus went sailing past. I had taken two buses to get to the doctor's office, determined to leave my car at home and do my part for the environment, theorizing that if I took care of Mother Nature, maybe she would take care of me. But now it was 4:00 and rush hour traffic was beginning to build. The journey could take as long as two hours, but all I was wanted was to be home.

I sat alone on the cold steel bench watching triple lines of traffic fly by me in both directions. Everyone was in a hurry; everyone was going somewhere, doing something, rushing, rushing, rushing, caught up in the rat race. I was in a rat race of my own, dashing from doctor to doctor, taking herbs and potions, eating sea cucumbers and quail eggs, gathering information, searching, questioning, trying, trying, trying to solve the puzzle as to why I couldn't have a baby. In my determination to avoid the Crazy Train of Reproductive

Medicine, I had boarded another Crazy Train entirely; different train but just as crazy. I'd been so self-righteous about not falling into the IVF trap, I hadn't seen the new insanity I'd been caught up in. But now I'd had enough. I just wanted to go home.

My cell phone rang with Jose's special ring. On our first anniversary trip to Carmel, we'd used that ring as an alarm to wake us up for dinner after the long afternoons of making love and sleeping by the dying fire, wrapped in one another's arms. It was a barnyard ring tone and we'd lain there together, trying to identify the different animal sounds. We'd laughed and listened to it over and over again because I had sworn I could hear a duck in the mix, but Jose was sure I was imagining the quack.

Sitting at the bus stop I heard the ring and thought about that trip. It had been less than three years ago, but it felt like a lifetime. I'd almost forgotten how making love with Jose had once been.

"I don't want to do this anymore," I told Jose when I answered the phone. "I'm tired of doctors and pills and of trying month after month and getting nowhere. I miss just spending time with you. I miss making love just because I love you and not because we're trying to make a baby. I just don't want to do this anymore."

"Then don't," he said. His voice was gentle, but sure.

I whimpered into the phone, "But..." but I had no further objections. We didn't have to do this. I'd be okay if I never had a baby, wouldn't I? An empty feeling filled my stomach at the thought. What if I never knew what it was like to have a baby growing inside me? What if I never looked into my own eyes and felt the love that can only exist between a mother and child? What would happen to me if I never became a mother?

But what would happen to Jose and me if we just kept on trying? Another year had passed and we were no closer to having a baby, and Jose and I were growing further and further apart. We both knew it. We were sailing on different tacks. Up close it appeared as if we were moving along side-by-side, both headed in the same direction, but the farther we traveled, the more that slight difference in tack pulled us apart. If we kept going, we'd soon lose sight of one another. We had to do something or we'd lose one another forever.

We weren't ready to give up on having children, but we had to step away from this insanity. I'd thought I could stay in control, but it felt as if every answer I got generated two more questions, which required two more tests, with two more answers, each generating two more questions. It was an endless cycle and we had to break it. We couldn't erase the past or the knowledge we'd accumulated, but we had to find a way to clear our minds and hearts, and figure out how to start again.

It was Jose's idea to try a Wiccan cleansing ceremony. Neither of us knew what that entailed, but it sounded like something that would clear out all the negative energy that had built up around us, force out all the demons we'd collected, and maybe give us a fresh start. It was no wackier than anything else we'd tried and, at the very least it would be a symbolic gesture of "this is where it ends; this is where something new begins," even if we didn't know what that something new might be. It was the perfect way to deal with our decision—by sweeping it away and not dealing with it at all.

We found instructions for the ceremony on the Internet, and on New Year's Eve I went to our local New Age bookstore to shop for the tools we'd need—a bunch of sage for smudging and a white candle. The owner recognized me; the last time I'd been in there I'd had to ask her if it was the red or the black penis-shaped candle I needed for fertility.

"Are you trying to get pregnant or trying not to?"

she'd asked. Two other women at the counter had stopped their conversation to wait for my response.

"Trying to," I'd said, slightly embarrassed.

"Red!" all three of them had chorused.

This time I selected my sage and plain white candle quickly, and left.

That night, Jose and I turned down the lights and lit candles all around the house. By the light of the white candle, Jose read the instructions while I performed the ceremony. First I swept all the negative forces from our house using the bristle broom we kept in the kitchen. It was a symbolic sweep, brushing all the built-up negative energy from the corners of our house and out the front door. I was surprised at how much had accumulated. Next I wafted smoke from the burning sage around all the rooms to cleanse away any bad spirits, and finally I took the white candle and, reading an incantation, I traced a pentagram across every door and window, sealing the house from evil spirits. Of all the desperate things we had tried, it was this ceremony that left us feeling most calm and most hopeful for our future. There was peace in performing a ritual, even an unconventional one. We had performed the ceremony ourselves, rather than submit to the powers of a practitioner, and it felt as if we were finally being proactive.

Most of all though, in sweeping the house and repeating the incantation, Jose and I had worked together as a team and as the New Year rang in, we saw an inkling of the Jose and Lisa we had once been.

10
Shopping for Karma
Year 4

One morning that spring, Jose and I went for a bike ride. We were trying hard to rekindle all the things we'd once loved to do together, and biking was one of our favorites. It was one of the many things we could easily do as a couple without children. We could just go—head out somewhere fun and see what came our way. This morning I was tired and felt as if I might be getting sick, but I knew better than to wonder if I might be pregnant. After just a couple of miles, we turned around and stopped for lunch. As I sipped my minestrone soup, I gazed out of the large restaurant window at the steady stream of strolling locals and tourists that drifted by, and saw a familiar figure passing by—my ex-fiancé, Mark. I didn't see him in detail, but I saw enough—his favorite blue fleece jacket, the long red hair of the woman beside him, and the sage green baby stroller that rolled along ahead of them.

The sound of Jose's voice blurred into a white buzz that filled my ears as if I had slipped underwater with a heavy weight tied to my ankle. The sights, the sounds, and smells of the restaurant around me slid into a swirling grey mist until all I could see down the narrow tunnel of clarity was the sage green baby stroller. I couldn't see the baby, couldn't tell if it was a boy with his daddy's chocolate eyes and thin pointed face or a little girl who had her mommy's fair complexion and had been named Julianna for her great-grandmother. All I knew is that the baby should have been mine.

I felt my face flush in anger and my chest squeezed so tight I couldn't breathe. Mark had wasted five years of my life insisting he didn't want children and now I was 37 and unable to conceive. Somehow, in that moment of my logic, my reproductive difficulties were all Mark's fault. Here was someone who'd never wanted children, proudly parading his offspring, while I, who dearly wanted a baby, was being denied the chance. He didn't deserve it. It should have been me.

"Are you okay?" Jose's warm familiar voice pulled me back to reality.

I looked up into his concerned face, the face I woke up to every morning, the one that broke so easily into unbridled laughter, the one that was so generous with its perfect kisses. I nodded and came back to my senses. I knew I didn't belong in a relationship with Mark. He'd offered me the chance of a family and I'd turned it down. I wanted a family with Jose, and no matter what we had been through and what we might still have to go through, this was where I was supposed to be. This was where I wanted to be, no matter what.

Still, it wasn't fair.

I stewed over the injustice for several weeks, flip-flopping between convincing myself that Mark had been coerced into fatherhood and thrashing myself for passing up the opportunity to have children with him. I'd think about Jose and remember why I was with him now and not with Mark. Then I'd think about being deprived of my chance at motherhood, and the cycle would begin again.

At one point during my treatments with Laura, she had suggested I try to focus my attention *outside* myself and my own circumstances. She thought that channeling positive energy elsewhere would be good for me, and suggested supporting a friend who was also trying to get pregnant. This seemed like a good time to test her theory.

Most of my friends already had children, but the one friend who I knew was venturing out on the road to motherhood was Cassie—the woman who had initially connected me with Laura. She and her husband had recently moved back to Los Angeles from New York and I took that to be a sign that she was ready to get serious about starting a family. I made plans to meet her for lunch, ready to be her cheerleader and focus all my baby attention on her.

Cassie looked great. It had been almost a year since I'd seen her and the fresh East Coast air seemed to have done her a world of good. Her skin glowed and she looked happy and relaxed. I noticed she was carrying a few extra pounds these days, but it suited her and she carried it well. We took a corner table at the little French cafe, ordered our food, and got down to the business of catching up. We talked about New York and how she was glad to be back in L.A.; we talked about our work and the projects we were working on; and then the subject turned to babies.

"What's going on with you?" she asked.

I updated her on the latest string of doctor sagas and how we'd decided to take a break.

"So, are you done?" she asked.

I shrugged. It was too complicated a situation for a simple response. We were done for now, but not forever, although we had no idea what our next move was going to be. "What about you?" I asked. I tried to keep in mind what Laura had said and tried to push my own story aside and focus all my positive energy onto Cassie and her journey. "Now you're back, are you officially trying?"

A strange look came over Cassie's face. It was almost a smile, with a hint of consolation, a smidgen of frown, and a dash of grimace. It was then that I realized she was already pregnant. My eyes flickered down to the waistline of her black wrapover dress and landed squarely on her slightly swollen belly. "Oh that's great," I said out loud. "Congratulations!" But behind my smile I was wondering what I had done to the Universe to turn it against me like this—and what I was going to do to turn it back in my favor.

I didn't subscribe to the true Buddhist belief in Karma—the idea that every action is repaid to you in this life or the next—but I had a vague notion that if I treated people well, in general, people would be good to me. If I did good deeds and lived in respect of others, that behavior would come back to me in the form of luck or kindness or friendship or love. And maybe if I was a nice person, I'd get to have a baby. But logic dictated that if I was unable to get pregnant, I must have done something in my past to hurt someone or something. I began sifting through my life trying to find a clue. I thought about the boyfriends I'd dumped and whose hearts I'd broken. They had been temporary heartbreaks, though, and I hadn't been such a great catch that any of them had been unable to recover from losing me. In fact, recent evidence suggested that they were getting along just fine without me—one might even say thriving. I thought about friends I'd neglected, unkind things I'd said, and feelings I might have hurt. There wasn't much to go on there either. Then my thoughts landed on Jose's ex-wife. He had told me they'd been emotionally separated for years before we'd met and that our meeting was just a catalyst for him leaving—something he would have done eventually anyway. At the time I'd believed him and absolved myself of all guilt, but in hindsight that had been simply out of convenience. Now, looking for a reason why the Universe would deprive me of motherhood, I saw myself clearly as a scarlet woman. Jose might have seen the demise in their relationship coming, but his ex-wife certainly hadn't. She'd had plans to retire to the desert, to quit her job and live out her days in quiet relaxation, but by leaving her as a single woman, Jose had taken that away from her. No, I had taken that away. I had stolen another woman's husband, a woman who had given 27 years of her life and raised his two children. And this was why the Universe had taken motherhood from me. I was getting exactly what I deserved.

There are some people who believe that there can be no rehabilitation for hardened criminals, that someone who has committed a serious crime cannot redeem himself by acknowledging his sins and working to keep others from making the same mistakes. I am not one of those people. I had committed adultery; I had coveted (and won) a married man, and now I needed redemption.

I found exactly what I needed on the website of my local hospital. They offered an extensive volunteer program where I could help out in all facets of hospital life. But what I wanted most of all was their Neonatal Intensive Care Unit's Cuddler Program. Here was a chance to do something good and show the Universe that I was worthy of motherhood by taking care of other people's babies. I called the Volunteer Services Office and signed up for the next orientation.

I immediately felt the positive energy that permeated the conference room where the orientation was held. The room was filled with kind souls, all looking for a way to give back, and I was glad to be doing something positive and useful. It was no longer all about me; it was about others who needed my help. I pictured myself as some sort of angel of mercy, striding down the hallways in my regulation blue smock and white pants, taking charge of urgent situations, acting on orders, doing good. But when we were asked to go around the room and tell the group why we had decided to volunteer, I was forced to admit, at least to myself, my true motives.

When I was a child, my mother had collected Green Shield stamps. I'd help her stick them into books, and when the books were full we'd take them into the store in town and exchange them for something she needed— new towels, a hand mixer—or sometimes something I wanted—a book or clothes for my doll. Now I was hoping to collect karma points, hoping to do enough good to collect sufficient points to get the thing I wanted most—a baby. I couldn't admit my ulterior motives to this room full of kindhearted souls. Doing so would acknowledge that I was sick, selfish, and twisted, that I was doing this in the hopes of getting something in return. It was in complete opposition to the spirit of volunteerism, so instead I told a version of the truth, which was that I needed to do something worthwhile, that I'd been fortunate in my life and felt I should do something important to give back.

Everyone else in the room had their own reasons for being there. They told of scrapes with death, serious illness and accidents, or a close call for a loved one. They were thankful for their survival and needed a way to show it. At first, their reasons seemed so much nobler than mine, but our intentions were the same; they got their karma on credit—I was simply paying for mine in advance.

Before I could get a permanent placement as a Cuddler, I had to complete a mandatory basic training period, where my duties involved running unpleasant-looking samples to the lab and wheeling discharged patients out to their cars. I was a good volunteer, a fast learner, willing to take even the most menial task and I looked forward to stepping into a role with more responsibility—and more babies.

It wasn't until my second shift in training that I was summoned to the maternity ward to discharge a new mother and her baby. I was excited and nervous. This was my chance to start proving my worth to the Universe, but it was also the first test of my mettle. Could I really be around newborn babies without having an emotional meltdown? I was about to find out. I took the elevator to the third floor, taking deep breaths and trying to keep my cool. I passed by the nursery window and glanced quickly at the tiny bundles wrapped in pink or blue blankets in their fish tank cribs. I felt my chest tighten but I breathed hard and pushed the lump of emotion away. I went to the room I'd been told, knocked gently on the door, and introduced myself. I cooed at the baby, commented on how beautiful she was, and told her two (very ornery-looking) older brothers to be good to their little sister. I kept breathing as I wheeled the mother out to her car, helped her out of her wheelchair and waved good-bye to the family. I was determined to be brave, to be an adult about this. *This is how life is,* I told myself. *You don't always get what you want.* I couldn't begrudge people their babies, just because I didn't have mine. So when the next mommy-baby discharge call came in, I was the first to volunteer.

On the following Saturday, when I put up my hand and said I'd step in to hand out fresh-baked chocolate chip cookies to all the new moms, a thought crept into my mind: *How hard would it be to grab a baby and make a run for it?* And as I wheeled my cart from one private room to the next, handing out cookies and cooing at sleeping bundles, I pictured myself fleeing down the hallway, lights flashing and the emergency warning system yelling "Code pink, code pink!" I started searching everything I knew about the security system, testing the fence for weakness, like a caged wild animal. I made calculations about how I could get away with suddenly arriving home with a baby. Would Jose be a willing accomplice, or would he be an upstanding citizen and turn me, and my baby, in? As I handed out the last cookie, I decided that Jose would try to talk me into doing the right thing. He'd force me to think about the poor mother and then he'd ask me to think if what I'd done was the best thing for the baby. And then he'd drive me to the hospital to give the baby back. For once I wished I'd married a more unscrupulous man.

By the time I graduated from training I was ready to take a post in the NICU. There was only one shift available for a Cuddler: 6 a.m. on Thursdays. The following week I dragged myself out of bed before dawn, put on my uniform and went off to the hospital to cuddle other people's babies.

My role as a Cuddler was to comfort premature or sick babies so that they could expend all their energy into growing and healing. Sleeping babies were off-limits, but fussy, restless babies needed to be held and comforted until they went back to sleep. I'd always had a knack for soothing crying babies and considered the skill to be something of a badge of honor, proof that I would make an excellent mother. I flourished as a Cuddler, and fell in love with another baby every time I worked. They were so tiny and fragile that I could barely feel some of them in my arms. I held them gently and hummed songs or talked to them, telling them all about the wonderful lives they would have as soon as they were big enough to go home. And I knew they would go home, because I saw the tireless care they received from the hospital staff, and the love they were given by the other volunteers. Still, I couldn't help but wonder about their stories. A small tag on the side of each crib told the baby's name, birth weight, current weight, and current gestational age, had they not been born before their time. I was amazed to see babies who had been born as early as 26 weeks—more than three months premature—grow strong and healthy. I watched the dedication of the parents, visiting two or three times a day, sometimes with older children—to feed, change and hold their babies.

There were two NICU units in the hospital. The Cuddlers worked mainly in the graduation unit with the babies who were almost well enough to go home, but sometimes we were sent to the other unit, with the smallest, sickest babies. These babies were impossibly tiny, barely formed into human beings. Their thin bodies were still covered with the light fuzz that usually disappeared at gestation. Their tiny forms lay in the center of enormous incubators, hooked up to machines and tubes designed to keep them breathing, keep their hearts beating, to keep them alive long enough to pass into the safe zone. But no one knew the future of these babies. They had been born much too early, long before their organs had fully developed, and those that graduated to the next NICU level faced a constant barrage of tests and medications, possibly for the rest of their lives.

For a number of weeks I cared for twin girls who had been born at 26 weeks and had been in the hospital for three months already. The older one was expected to go home at any time, but the younger one was struggling. She was often cranky and when her eyes opened, they never seemed to fully focus, wavering back and forth, and there was concern that her brain had not fully developed. I watched one day as her nurse changed her diaper and clothes. She slid the miniature t-shirt over the baby's head and I had to suppress a gasp. Down the front of the baby's little pink chest ran a long ugly scar. Already in her short life she had undergone heart surgery and she faced more medical procedures down the road.

I couldn't help but wonder how many of the babies in the unit had been conceived by IVF. In a unit with no more than ten beds at any one time, there were always two or three sets of twins. I knew that twins were often naturally premature, but that there were so many twins at one time gave me pause. I thought back to Doctor Hassan and all the drugs I'd been told I would have to take to force my body into getting and staying pregnant. Jose and I had discussed in the beginning the realities of having a sick child. We had agreed that even if in utero tests showed mental or physical disabilities, we would choose to have that child regardless, and to love him no matter what. But if I had forced that child into existence, using drugs and medical miracles, would I be able to live with the consequences? I knew I would have to, but seeing so many sick children only caused me to further question the safety and ethics of assisted reproduction. Even though I didn't have a baby of my own, I knew I'd made the right decision for me.

Jose thought I was insane to take the Cuddler job. I'd done a pretty good job of maintaining a brave face in public, and he was the only person who'd really seen the level of my frustration. He'd mopped up countless tears of frustration over the past three-and-a-half years. Every month, when it hadn't worked again, I'd tried to pretend it was okay, but it wasn't and sooner or later I would have to let it out. I hadn't been to a baby shower in three years, never sure if I'd make it through the celebration without my chest tightening and my voice cracking. I'd opted to send gifts instead, resorting ultimately to shopping online so as not to lose it again in the furniture section of Babies "R" Us. It was easy to see how "bitter" and "childless" often ended up in a sentence together, and I was determined that if I had to be one of those things, I wasn't going to be both. I'd always thought of myself as a strong woman, never the one sniffling into a Kleenex in public. If I was going to overcome my demons, I was going to have to face them dead-on. Cuddling other people's babies was torturous, but I wanted to prove I could do it. I wanted to test my resolve, to see how strong I really was. But before long I realized that this was more than putting on a brave face, more even than proving I was worthy of motherhood. I was punishing myself for being unable to conceive. Cuddling babies was my hair shirt and I wore it proudly. I suffered the pain with my chin held high—Saint Lisa, the infertility martyr.

Over the summer I got to play mother again when my 16-year-old nephew and his friend came from England to spend a month with us. I was nervous at first, worried about the responsibility of taking care of someone else's kids and concerned about where the boundaries between parent, temporary caretaker, and Weird Childless Aunt overlapped. I didn't believe, for example, that it was my place to talk to them about sex and the fact that the age of consent in the U.S. is 18 and not 16, as in the U.K. Then I imagined having to make the phone call to their parents to explain that they'd been arrested for underage sex because they were unfamiliar with the law. We made a decision and Jose provided contingency condoms and some man-to-man advice.

Despite my lack of hands-on training, I took to motherhood with great enthusiasm, cooking copious amounts of high carbohydrate foods, sifting endless piles of dirty laundry, and planning outings and activities. I tried to take a cool, aunt-like liberal view towards independence and self-sufficiency, letting them loose on bikes and the L.A. public transportation system, even agreeing to let them travel home alone via Amtrak from our trip to San Francisco, but I was terrified of something happening to them every time they left the house.

During our stay in San Francisco, we rented bikes for a day and pedaled out of town and across the Golden Gate Bridge. I yelled, "Be careful," so many times that I should have had it recorded to save my voice. Finally, as they went flying ahead of me down the narrow two-lane road into Sausalito, I rode behind with my heart up in my mouth, gasping and squeaking in fear with every passing car. When I yelled, "slow down," for about the 47th time, my nephew turned back and rolled his eyes at me, "You're having a heart attack over nothing," he said and rode away, leaving me feeling as if I were 100 years old. From that point on, I decided to relax my reins and just enjoy the experience of being a temporary mother.

For a month, my house was full of large smelly feet and long hairy legs, and the kitchen had a new permanent fixture—the dirty pizza pan. My guest room had approximately two square feet of visible carpet and my fridge bore a striking resemblance to Old Mother Hubbard's cupboard. But my house was also full of laughter. We (eventually) laughed at my nephew's horrific sunburn that left him the color of medium-rare roast beef with a horseradish white bow pattern on his stomach, from the string of his shorts. The boys were elevated from something of a nerdy status in their hometown to movie star repute here. "Oh my God! You're from England?!" was a cry we heard from several teenage girls. "Say something in English!" At which point, the boys pulled out their best accents and said things like, "Jumper, rubbish, and tomato (to-*mar*-to, as opposed to to-*may*-to)." We had hearty dinner table debates, with Jose taking a contrary point-of-view, just to spark an argument. Sometimes, when we were out walking together I'd imagine they were my sons and I'd soak up the feelings of pride and warmth that ran through me. I loved it. I loved the responsibility, the annoyance, the smells, and the laughter, and after they'd returned home to their real mothers, the house felt empty. Jose felt it too. As we were sitting on opposite couches reading our books, he looked up at me. "It's quiet around here, isn't it?" I nodded. "Glad to have the house to ourselves again?" he asked.

I shook my head. "Not really."

"Me neither."

"It was fun having kids," I said.

He nodded. "We'll get some of our own soon," he said.

I believed him, but I didn't know how it was going to happen. Borrowing was only temporary, stealing was out of the question, and, despite recently reading two novels involving unwanted babies left on doorsteps, I was pretty sure that wasn't going to happen to me. So, it was with great resolve and firmly drawn boundaries that I made an appointment with the new fertility doctor that the urologist had recommended. This time we were armed with knowledge and experience. We knew what we wanted, what to ask for, and how far we were willing to go. This time we were ready.

11
Breasts

When I was 15, a man in a store had called me "son" and my cruel friends teased me mercilessly for weeks. By the time I hit 17, there was no disputing my womanliness in my long limbs and pert little boobs. It took a few more years and a few extra pounds for my body to divulge all its feminine curves and for me to proudly refer to the appendages on the front of my chest as breasts. I thought they were beautiful—tender, pert, feminine, a part of me for which I was grateful. I no longer called them by any of their derogatory alternatives—tits, boobs, mammaries, knockers, or rack; they were my breasts and I was proud of them.

But now they were utterly useless.

At least according to Doctor Forester, the new Reproductive Endocrinologist we went to see. He came highly recommended and had begun to restore our faith in reproductive medicine. He had listened carefully to our story and agreed to start with a simple program of Intrauterine Insemination in the hopes of getting Jose's sperm closer to my eggs, but after four rounds it hadn't worked. He strongly recommended that we move forward with IVF, but we stuck to our decision. I didn't want the drugs and I didn't want the quick fix; I needed to understand *why* it wasn't working. Doctor Forester conducted another series of tests and a pelvic ultrasound gave us our answer.

"You only have one producing follicle on each ovary," he said.

My mind shut down, overwhelmed by this information I couldn't fully comprehend, but I watched dumbly as the doctor took a Post-It and sketched my ovary with its single follicle and then highlighted the problem by adding the six to ten additional follicles he would normally expect to see. "Your chances of becoming pregnant with IVF would be about 25 percent."

I stared at the sketch trying to absorb this information, trying to reconcile the flying nuggets of information—IVF, one follicle, 25 percent—with my overriding conviction that IVF was not an option for me, and slowly reaching the conclusion that the procedure I had so vehemently opposed was no longer even a viable option.

"Using donor eggs would give you about a 50 percent success rate," said the doctor.

And that was that. In his quiet matter-of-fact way, the doctor told me that I would never have a biological child of my own. Never. My only option for pregnancy was to use someone else's eggs, not my eggs, a stranger's eggs. My genetic line would end with me.

My ears filled with a grey roar and, just before my mind went blank, the word *Chernobyl* flashed across it one more time. In the background, the doctor was still talking, explaining something called Fragile X, a genetic disorder of which poor ovarian function is a symptom and which can cause mental retardation in children. He strongly recommended we test for the gene before proceeding.

In a trance, I followed him and before I knew it, I was at the nurse's station again with my sleeve rolled up, ready to give another vial of blood to test for Fragile X. As the nurse tied the tourniquet around my arm, the snap of the latex brought me back. Something in my brain clicked into place and I changed my mind. *This is where it stops*, I thought. In that second I knew that I would never have a baby. I knew it without a doubt. I didn't yet know how I would deal with this knowledge, but I knew I had reached the end of the line. There would be no IVF, no donor eggs, and no pregnancy for me. I rolled down my sleeve and told the nurse I'd do the test some other time, but meant I'd do it never.

"This was the last thing I expected to hear today," Jose said as we collapsed into a quiet corner booth at Marie Callender's. We'd left the doctor's office in stunned silence, not knowing what to do next, or even where to go. Finally, Jose had suggested going for pie. Forgetting that I didn't really like pie, I had followed along.

Jose looked as if he'd been flattened by a steamroller. "It's the last thing I expected to hear," he said again.

"Donor eggs," I said, shaking my head. "What's the bloody point?"

I could feel a ball of fury building inside me. Someone ought to have looked at this years ago and saved us all the heartache. All the doctor's appointments I'd been to, all the tests I'd done, all the money I'd spent, why did no one figure this out before now? What if we'd bought the first fertility doctor's sales pitch and signed up for his deal? How many rounds of IVF would we have gone through before he'd admitted that my eggs weren't up to the task of reproduction? How many others had taken that route only to find themselves where we stood now?

Mainly, though, I was angry with myself. I should have pushed for more tests sooner; I should have listened to the urologist and eliminated myself as the problem; I should have listened to my instincts. I could feel the fury mounting, but I was too exhausted, and what was the point? I could be as angry as I wanted; it wasn't going to change what had happened. Instead I felt numb and sad. I ought to have been devastated, but I wasn't. In hindsight, in my gut, I had known this day was coming. How many times had I been asked, "Have you been tested yet?" But I'd brushed away the thought, hanging my hat on the fact that Jose was the problem, unable to face the possibility that my body might not be working as intended. And yet in the back of my mind I had known. The Reiki Master I'd visited had made a point of telling me that her hands had been drawn to my ovaries, and since then, I had known that a diagnosis like this was coming. But I'd kept my eye on my dream, held onto my belief that I was destined to become a mother. Acknowledging my instinct that there might be something wrong with me would have meant accepting the possibility of failure, admitting that I might not get things my way. The signs were all there, but I chose to ignore them. My subconscious, however, had been reading the signs and anticipating my inability to reproduce. It was because of this, I think, that I took the news with stalwart acceptance.

Not so Jose. He looked as if someone had sucked all the air out of him, washed him in too hot water, and hung him out to dry by the scruff of his neck. I gave him a lopsided smile to convince him it would be okay.

"It's so unfair," he said.

He was right about that. He had been through microsurgery, acupuncture, and general indignity—and all for someone with bum ovaries. All he'd wanted was for me to have a child of my own, to experience pregnancy and to have the chance to be a mother to our child, but that chance was gone. He had given everything he could so that I could have what I wanted and in the end I had let him down. I had pushed and pushed, promising that, if I could just have this one thing, I'd be good. I'd made a secret pact with myself that once I got my baby I would make it up to Jose for everything he'd done for me. I'd be the best wife a man could ever wish for. I'd bend over backwards to make his life comfortable and easy. I'd support him emotionally and financially so he could go back to school, and I'd never ask for anything again. But I hadn't held up my end of the bargain and everything he'd been through had been for nothing.

I felt utterly drained, as if I'd traveled for four years on an arduous journey only to find myself arriving at the wrong destination. There was none of the jubilation of a warm welcome, the comfort of finally being home. If I'd been told I was pregnant, the whole journey would have been worthwhile, but this.... It all felt like such a waste of our lives.

I tried to be angry. I tried to provoke myself into a fury by calling myself names, telling Jose that from now on I would refer to myself as "a barren, old broad." I played a game where I typed *barren* and *infertile* into my computer's thesaurus and followed through on the different meanings to see where they led. *Barren* generated *desolate, bleak, austere,* and *inhospitable.* The words conjured up the rugged backdrop of a Brontë novel and the pinched, hard face of the resident old spinster, bent on directing her resentment for her own unfulfilled existence on the sweet, hapless heroine. *Infertile* turned up *unfruitful* and *unproductive,* which in turn led to *idle, wasteful, futile,* and *pointless.* That was exactly how I felt.

I'd always believed that being a woman was never a

handicap; I could do anything I chose to do, even if tradition deemed it inappropriate. But the one thing I was expected to do, not only by society, but also by Mother Nature, was to reproduce. As a woman, my *raison d'etre*, my purpose, was to bear children, to produce the next generation of humankind. If women did not reproduce, there would be no future for our species. It was my job to contribute to the continuation of my kind, and I had failed. Did that mean that I was no longer a real woman? Was I still a valuable part of the human race if I didn't contribute to its future? I knew the answer, just as Rosa Parks, Amelia Earhart, and Dian Fossey had known. Louisa May Alcott, Julia Child, even Oprah Winfrey had never raised children either, but no one could claim that they had contributed nothing to society.

I knew I wasn't taking up valuable oxygen on the planet if I didn't have children, but I didn't know what it would mean if our family consisted only of Jose and me. We'd made it this far together—we'd had enough in common to get us together in the first place—and that ought to be enough to keep us going. But for an entire lifetime? I thought about all the milestone moments in a typical family: the Christmases, the graduations, the weddings, the births of the next generation. We'd miss all those, and even though I'd never hinged my whole existence on those events, what would our lives be like without them? And what would happen to Jose and me in our old age? What would happen to me if I was alone?

I remembered having a conversation about this with my mother years ago, before infertility was a word I'd ever used.

"You shouldn't have children just so you won't be alone," she had said.

"Oh I know," I had told her. "It wouldn't be my reason to have children, but it's certainly a consideration."

I thought again about my uncle and how he had to rely on my mother, aunts and cousins to care for him. And my godmother who had never married or had children. She counted on her two grown nieces to provide her family community. But I lived 6,000 miles away from my family; I had no blood relatives here. I didn't know what would become of me if I went into old age alone.

There was a positive side to being childless, though. I thought about my friends whose lives revolved entirely around their children. They spent their days shuttling their kids from school to dance classes to homework. Their children governed their weekends, their vacations, everything they did. The women I had known, before the children came along, had gone, leaving no evidence that they had ever existed. I'd seen dreams not merely put on hold, but put away for ever, never to be brought out again. I had a friend with an incredible talent for spotting up-and-coming musicians, but with a 10-year-old daughter to care for, she could see no way of turning her passion into a career. I had friends who wanted to finish college, even went back to school to take a class or two, but sooner or later, family intruded and those dreams were put back on ice.

But I was no different. I had already put my life on hold in the pursuit of having a baby. For the past four years my entire focus, everything in my life, had revolved around creating a new life. The food I ate, the activities I participated in, even the trips I took, all took into consideration the possibility of me becoming pregnant, or of having a child to include in my plans. Our lives as they'd once been had been put on hold and I could no longer clearly remember the people we used to be or see the people we might be in the future.

It was hard to think about the future after all we'd been through. I had never really imagined a life with

Jose that didn't include children. I could clearly visualize our coal-haired baby growing into a beautiful little boy or girl. I had envisioned trips to England to see my family, showing our children all my favorite places and telling them stories about my dad and grandparents, all the people they would never be able to meet. I could picture the day-to-day madness and joy of raising children; even picture the tantrums, the vomiting, the issues at school, the fights among siblings. But I'd never pictured my future without children.

Now, free from the responsibility of motherhood, I could be anything I wanted to be. I would have no children to tie me to home or even to country. I could do as I pleased, go where I wanted, and be whoever I wanted to be—but I no longer knew what that was. I tried to think back to the list of dreams Jose and I had once written. Mount Everest, South Africa, Egypt, the Taj Mahal. If I concentrated hard I could imagine trekking to the base camp of Mount Everest and looking up at the glittering summit of the highest point in the world. I could picture us buying a small boat and setting sail around the world, cruising into exotic ports and living the local life until the winds called and we set sail again. I could imagine all manner of adventures without the responsibility of children in tow, but when I thought about never holding my child's hand, never having someone who loved me without question climb into my lap for comfort, never holding a small person who was solely dependent on me, my heart lurched and sunk heavy in my chest. All the desire that I'd hoarded over the years came rushing at me, sweeping me away and out to sea, where I would bob around aimlessly waiting to be rescued by my fantasy of motherhood. I'd be bobbing for a very long time.

Even though I couldn't imagine my life without children in it, there was nothing I could do to prevent that life from happening. My body was unable to perform the one function for which it was designed. The very core of my being was broken and no matter how strong I made the rest of myself, that part of me, and all that it represented, had malfunctioned. As a woman, I was incomplete. I would never be a mother.

And so my breasts became useless appendages. They had been designed to provide nourishment for my offspring, but there would be no offspring to nourish, and so they became merely interesting accessories. As my next period approached, my breasts reminded me of their presence by swelling to what felt like twice their normal size and aching from somewhere deep inside my body. The tenderness eased with the arrival of my period, but that only served to accentuate the fact that my breasts were superfluous. Period equals not pregnant equals no babies equals no good use for my breasts. And no good use for me.

12
Crazy Train: Ticket for One
Year 5

E very day at work I began hearing the same public
service announcement. A young man was thanking
his dad for being a great father, and it was clear they
were part of a perfect family unit. The announcer gave
an 800 number to call and a website to visit, but it wasn't
until I'd heard the commercial for several weeks that I
actually listened and realized it was promoting adoption
of foster children.

Adoption had always been part of my motherhood
fantasy, rather than a last resort. Jose and I had discussed
it long ago, but over the past four years I'd learned more
about the process and I realized it wasn't the simple,
surefire solution I'd once thought. I'd met people who'd
traveled to foreign countries only to have the laws
change on them, or to find themselves the victims of
corrupt officials. Domestic adoption was no less of a
minefield and I'd heard firsthand stories of couples
"auditioning" to be adoptive parents for an unborn child,
providing financial support for the birth mother—and
father—only to be "dropped" at the last second. It wasn't
an avenue I wanted to pursue and I was surprised to

hear a commercial promoting an option that was already oversubscribed. Eventually, though, I realized that the campaign was promoting adoption of older children from foster care. I wrote down the website and that night, before Jose got home from work, I tapped in the URL.

The site was designed to guide potential parents through the adoption process and connect them with adoption agencies in their area. The average age of the children seeking adoption was eight. That wasn't going to fulfill my desire for a baby, but it would still allow me to be a mother. And wasn't that what it was really all about? My curiosity was piqued and I felt a shift in my attitude. So what if I never had a baby of my own? Who needed all that agony, all that bloating and those stretch marks? Maybe I could get what I wanted some other way. I thought I could be a wonderful mother to an adopted child.

I clicked through to the California agency's site until I came across a link for a photo gallery of children awaiting adoption. I didn't want to click through. I was afraid of having to face the reality of our world, that there are children who are mistreated and unwanted, who don't get to live the kind of life a child deserves. But I couldn't close the window. I clicked on the link and up popped a laundry list of human beings—a gallery of children all looking for someone to love them and take care of them. They all needed a bedtime story or someone to brush the tangles out of their hair. They were children who'd lived most of their young lives in foster care, shuttling from one home to another, one school to another, always the new kid in class, the new kid on the street and the new kid in their home. Some of them had such severe disabilities that they would need full-time care for the rest of their lives, which could mean the rest of my life. I looked inside my own self and I was sorry to admit that I didn't find the necessary gumption to voluntarily take responsibility for a child with special needs. I wished I was a better person, or at least a stronger person, but I knew I was an honest person, even if I didn't like the truth.

I scrolled down the list of children and opened up the page for a boy named Darrell. Darrell was 14 and came as a package with his 13-year-old brother D'Shaun. I looked at the dark, curled eyelashes and goofy grins of the two boys smiling out at me and I couldn't help but smile myself. Darrell played basketball and liked to draw; D'Shaun wrote poetry and enjoyed reading mystery novels. I pictured my house with these two boys in it and I felt that wave of maternal love flow over me again. In my fantasy Darrell was at the dining room table working on his homework; his best drawing was in a frame on the wall over the fireplace. D'Shaun had finished his homework already, so he was on the couch, his nose in a book, just like his new daddy. It was the perfect domestic scene.

I could picture myself sandwiched between these two beautiful smiles, although both boys would tower above their "Little Mom." I could see us at Darrell's high school graduation. He'd have plans to go to UCLA on a basketball scholarship, but he'd be studying fine arts, as we'd been told he had talent.

I shook off this ridiculous fantasy. I couldn't possibly take on two teenage boys. I'd done it before with my nephew and his friend—for a month. But mothering two boys from stable homes and loving families—families to which they could be shipped back if they misbehaved—was not the same as taking on strangers, whose history I knew nothing about. Did I really believe that love and laughter was enough to heal damage from abuse or a lifetime of instability? I didn't know the answer to that.

I closed down Darrell and D'Shaun's window. Even

if Jose and I began the adoption process today, it would be at least a year before we could take home a child and I was certain that Darrell and D'Shaun would find a loving home before then.

The boys didn't go far from my thoughts. A few days later the *LA Weekly* ran an article about foster children who fell out of the system at 18 and had nowhere to go. Darrell had four years until he was one of them. Could four years in a stable loving home get a boy like Darrell into college, or art school, or signed with the Lakers? It could at least get him off the streets.

The idea began to grow on me and I started to think about our quest to have a baby. Over the course of four years it had become a quest to get pregnant, to prove to the Universe that it was wrong to select me for the challenge of infertility and that 38 couldn't possibly be too old to reproduce. But I thought back to the infertility message boards and the woman with the 37 eggs and it hit me square between the eyes. A family wasn't just a by-product of getting pregnant—a family was the Holy Grail. Getting pregnant was a means to that end, but it wasn't the only means.

Adopting a child, even an older child would give us the family we wanted and take the pressure off our incessant quest for a baby. It would give us time to explore all the possibilities of alternative therapies that might help us create a child of our own, but adoption would give us the thing we truly desired—children. Maybe this was fate. Maybe I was destined to be an adoptive mother. I knew I could do this job and what's more, I wanted to.

I brought up the subject with Jose and he agreed. He was pragmatic about taking in foster children and some of the issues we might encounter, but he touted his own experience with teenagers as a plus. Over the next several days I noticed a lightness come over me. The fog of despair that had shrouded me for so long was clearing and I was filled with a beautiful sensation—hope.

On my daily walk to my job, I mulled the possibilities and imagined the challenges of adopting from foster care. I thought about the limitations of our two-bedroom house. We could afford to move to a bigger place if we moved inland, but leaving our great school district with teenage kids seemed foolish for the sake of an extra room. I'd have to change around my hours at work to be home when the kids got out of school. It would be important for them to know that I was there if they needed me. I was surprised and pleased that I was starting to think like a mom.

Not long after this, Adela came into my life.

She found me one day around the time I walked past Seaside Lagoon—a children's water area, closed now for the winter. I wasn't looking for her, not even especially thinking about her, but suddenly I felt her presence, as if it was where she was always supposed to be.

Adela was about eight years old. She had smooth mocha skin and long black hair, pulled haphazardly into lopsided pigtails. She looked at me for a moment, then smiled, revealing an empty space between the tiny squares of baby teeth. In my mind, I took her hand and she walked with me the rest of the way to work. She didn't say much, just skipped along beside me, but I could feel her warm hand in mine and it gave me comfort.

Adela and I spent as much time as we could together, but only when there was no one else around. When I ran at the beach in the mornings, I pictured her riding her bike beside me. She was still a little wobbly as she hadn't been riding for long, but suddenly she'd get a boost of confidence and sprint ahead of me, her pigtails flaring out behind her from underneath her pink helmet. At night, when I was sitting in my chair, she'd climb in beside me and we'd read a book together, or sometimes we'd each read our own books and she'd tap me now and again and ask me what a certain word meant, or how to say it.

Before long, I could picture Adela in every aspect of my life. I figured out my work schedule so that I could take her to school and be home for her afterwards. I made plans to rearrange the kitchen so I could help her with her homework while I made dinner. I looked for movies that would be appropriate for her to see and thought about family vacations where I could take her to the great outdoors. She would help me grow vegetables in the garden, takes dance classes on Thursdays, and would chose to paint her room Gypsy Pink. Her favorite shop would be Old Navy and her favorite food spaghetti with butter. Pretty soon I couldn't imagine my life without Adela in it. It was with this image planted clearly in my head that Jose and I embarked on our training to become foster parents and eventually to adopt.

Adela's sweet face was wiped from my imagination in the first class, when a thin, watery-eyed social worker told us "This is not for the faint of heart," and proceeded to show us a video of a typical foster family. I fell in love instantly with the preteen boy who arrived to stay with a friendly-looking retired couple. He was a sweet boy with a cheeky smile and I opened up a valve in my heart and imagined loving this boy. I kept turning up the love valve as the boy took out his anger on the woman's prize roses and locked himself in his room in a ball of fury. I mustered up all the tolerance I could find when the boy's biological father became abusive on his legal visitation and I tried to harden my heart and blink back tears when the boy was eventually taken away from that wonderful couple and returned to his mother. And all the while, I drummed up a mantra in my head, "I can do this, I can do this."

The following week, we did a role-playing exercise and I played the role of the birth mother, whose children were removed from my care and placed in foster homes. Because of certain circumstances my children were placed with different sets of foster parents, one of whom wanted to adopt my two-year-old daughter. Then the older daughter was abused while in care and was moved to yet another home. The story had a happy ending in that I got my children back (after a year!) but I came out of the exercise feeling utterly devastated. It was heartbreaking to have my children taken away and placed with strangers and even more distressing to see my children so upset and frightened.

I'd had a vision that Jose and I would be some kind of saviors, opening up our hearts and home to a child who would be grateful for a safe haven. But that child already had a home and a family; it was just that a judge had decided it was a bad home and so the child was uprooted from all that she knew and placed with strangers. And while I desperately wanted a child to adopt, all that child really wanted was to go back to her real family. Sometimes that happened and sometimes it didn't. All I knew for certain was that in order for something good to happen for Jose and me, something very bad had to happen to a whole string of people, but especially to the child.

Jose attended every class with me and participated in all the exercises and role-playing games, but I began to sense a change in his mood. Whereas I felt determined that I would make myself be strong enough to take on this role and hopeful that we would one day have a child, the feeling I got from him was reluctance, mixed with anger, frustration, maybe even fear. But whenever I questioned him, his response was the same. "We have to do this. Knowing what we know, how can we not?"

One hot Saturday afternoon we were in an air-conditioned classroom with a dozen other potential foster parents and the topic of the day was discipline. Nadine, the social worker, explained that children who have been hurt, whether physically or emotionally, cannot be parented in the same way as children who feel safe.

"When the child acts out," she said, "you can't raise your voice or simply tell them to stop. You have to tell them, 'I understand you're angry, so let's talk about this.'"

Beside me, I felt Jose bristle. I glanced at him, but his eyes were narrowed and focused directly on Nadine. Finally he raised his hand. "I understand that these kids have to be handled differently," he said, "but I've raised two kids and the methods you're suggesting sound like a recipe for disaster. Kids need boundaries and sometimes you just have to tell them to cut that out."

I was so proud of him for speaking up and I waited for Nadine to acknowledge his experience and make some concession. Instead, she took a defensive stance. She tossed her long hair over her shoulder and tilted her chin upwards. "And I'm sure your children turned out just fine, but this is different. There have been countless research papers written on raising the hurt child. You're going to have to unlearn everything you think you know."

I braced myself for Jose to blow. His distaste for Nadine had been slowly brewing and this insult had to be the last straw. I waited, but instead he said, "Then I'll defer to your expertise," and let it go.

Once in the car, he let it all hang out. "Countless studies," he said. "She can read all she damn well wants about raising kids, but as soon as you're in the trenches, all that goes out the window. She doesn't even have kids."

I bristled. I couldn't count the times that frustrated mothers had thrown that line at me, not intending to hurt, but stinging nonetheless. My intelligence and life experience were dismissed out-of-hand. I couldn't possibly offer anything constructive to the conversation, because I didn't have kids of my own. It was irrelevant that I'd read and listened, that I'd watched my brothers and then my friends raise their children and had paid close attention to what went right and what went wrong. It didn't matter that, because I *didn't* have kids, I could look at a situation objectively, from a place outside of the melee, something they were unable to do from inside the eye of the storm. Over time, I'd stopped expressing my opinions to avoid getting hurt. I couldn't take the chance of having the obvious pointed out to me—the fact that I didn't have children.

And now Jose was doing the same to Nadine, but still, I took his side. I understood that these children were different, but she had dismissed Jose's hands-on experience out of hand and that wasn't fair either.

Six weeks later we graduated from the class. Jose didn't get thrown out and in fact got the biggest round of applause on graduation day. With our certificates in hand, we were ready to start our home study and all the necessary paperwork.

Except we weren't ready at all. We were exhausted, mentally and emotionally drained from everything that we'd learned. "Knowing what we know now," repeated Jose, as if it was some kind of mantra, "we *have* to do this. How can we not?" All the same, we agreed to take an Adoption Vacation, for a month, just to let it all sink in and to steel ourselves for the next step.

Six months later, we were still on vacation. We had more than four years of trying to have a family behind us and we were staring at another long and difficult journey to adoption. Jose looked exhausted. He had gained weight and his face was puffy, with an odd yellow pallor. He took long naps every day after work and was cranky all the time. The stress was going to kill him, and I knew he didn't want to do this any more. But it was too hard to do without him and this was the only way I could see of getting my baby. I had to do this.

I made plans for us to meet my friend Diane for lunch. Diane was one of the very first friends I made when I moved to California. Over the years we'd weathered divorces, job issues, man issues, kids, step-kids, and even foster kids. Diane understood me, knew what made me tick, but wasn't afraid to give it to me straight if she thought I needed to hear it. She was also a product of the foster care system and knew exactly what we would be facing. I needed her to tell me it would be okay, that it would be a rewarding experience, and that I was strong enough to take on the challenge. We plied her with *moules-frites* and a bottle of good French wine and asked for her opinion.

"Don't do it," she said. "You're setting yourselves up for heartbreak."

I stared at her, incredulous that my friend wouldn't support our plans. I felt tears stinging my eyes and tried to blink them back, but they overflowed. I just left them to run their course.

"This won't get you what you want," she went on. "You want your little baby all of your own, but it's not your baby, it's someone else's, and it can be taken away from you in a flash. I know you. You're a good person and this is going to break your heart."

I excused myself from the table and locked the door of the ladies room behind me. My friend was wrong about me. She didn't know me at all. She saw me as some fickle creature who just wanted something cute to cuddle, but that wasn't me at all. I was strong and determined and I knew I was capable of taking on this challenge; I *wanted* to take on this challenge. But my husband was no longer with me. Jose had put his heart out, just as I had, and already it had been cracked and bruised. He didn't think he could stand to have it broken again if we fell in love with a child that we couldn't keep. And I didn't want to hurt him.

I stared at my face in the bathroom mirror. The features seemed unfamiliar to me. There was a hint of my brother around the eyebrows, the crease around my eyes like my other brother, my dad's nose and the shape of my mother's smile, but pieced together they made up the face of a stranger. This wasn't the face of a mother. It was the face of some unknown being that traveled the earth and didn't belong anywhere. It was the face of a woman without children, a woman whose body would not reproduce, a woman who wasn't strong enough to give a home to a hurt child, a woman who had failed at motherhood. She was a woman who was completely unrecognizable to me. In the past I'd imagined my face in pictures with children. That face was a soft face that crinkled around the eyes from laughing. It was a face that had survived sleepless nights and the eternal worry that comes with loving someone unconditionally. The face in the mirror was different. I no longer knew who this woman was. Whoever she was, I let her cry, and when she was done, she went back to the table and pretended she was hungry for dessert.

13
A New Life

Year 5

Jose was waiting for me when I walked out of the Delta Airlines terminal and back into the harsh L.A. sunlight. My nose was tan from the late summer sun and my hiking boots were dusty, the soles studded with shards of Italian dolomite. With my heavy backpack slung casually over one shoulder and my scraped and bruised knees evidence of my climbing a vertical rock face clipped only to a cable, I looked like a woman who had her life together. If I'd have seen myself, I'd have thought, *There goes just the kind of strong, no-nonsense woman I would like to be.*

Jose looked like a man who'd been living on frozen leftovers for two weeks while his wife went off hiking in the Italian Alps with her mother. It was the same look a Golden Retriever has every time his master comes home from work—a little sorry for himself for being left behind, but excited for what treats the immediate future might hold. I was glad to see him, too. The time spent alone with my mother, outdoors, doing what we loved, had brought us closer together and further cemented our mother-daughter bond. But I'd missed Jose. I'd missed our conversations, missed throwing together dinner while we talked. I'd missed his skin, too. I'd missed resting my head in the warm crook of his shoulder and pressing my cheek against the smooth bit where the hair stops. We'd made the decision that our little family would just be the two of us, and now we needed time to reconcile that decision. We needed to make peace with a future without children, and get to know one another again. In some ways letting go of the quest was a relief and I was looking forward to getting on with our lives.

Jose took my bag and carried it out to the parking lot. "So how was it?" he asked, and then let me ramble on about the pristine air, the jagged peaks, the death-defying climbs, and the sumptuous apple strudel. We navigated the parking structure and the treacherous inner ring road of L.A.'s International Airport, and were turning south onto Sepulveda Boulevard, before I stopped telling stories and asked, "So what's going on with you?"

"Not much," he said. "I've been fine. Ate most of the dinners you left, except the mystery ones."

I laughed. I'd labeled a supply of frozen leftovers in the freezer so that Jose could have "home-cooked" meals while I was gone. There had been a couple of frozen blocks I'd been unable to identify, but the fact that he'd eaten any of them and hadn't lived on takeout for two weeks was a great relief. I'd felt a pang of guilt about going on vacation without him, but he'd encouraged me to spend the time with my mum, and I'd been grateful for the chance to get away from anything relating to babies.

"I have a bit of news," he said, as the signal turned to green and he eased the car out into the flow of traffic.

I cocked my head, wondering if his dad was okay, if

his sister was in trouble, or if his job was in jeopardy.

"Penny's going to have a baby," he said.

There was perhaps a second of silence while my brain processed this unexpected news, and then my stomach shriveled into a dark knotted ball and my heart beat extra hard, pushing anger and malice out into my bloodstream and around to every cell of my body. My husband's daughter was pregnant, which meant only one thing to me: my stepdaughter was going to be a mother and I was not. My mind scrambled through a selection of appropriate responses, but instead, "Is it Travis'?" was the thought that bubbled to the top of the list and was out of my mouth before I could stop it. I regretted it instantly, but it was too late. My husband had told me his only daughter was going to be a mother, and I had questioned her fidelity.

Jose gave a half-laugh. "Yes, it's Travis'."

I nodded, checking my mental list again for the next appropriate thing to say, but it was hard. None of the things I wanted to say were at all appropriate. I didn't know if this was something Penny was happy about, or if Jose was happy, or if this was the biggest disaster to ever have befallen any of them.

"Is this a good thing?" I ventured.

"It's a good thing," he said, nodding his head like he believed it but knew I didn't. "So let it be good."

I was stung by his insinuation that I might react badly to the news, that I might take this happy occasion and wreck it because of my own selfish needs. I pasted a sweet smile on my face. "Of course," I said, holding every fiber of my body as still as possible, lest I shake loose any fragment of true emotion.

How could this be happening to me? Why had the Universe seen fit to deprive me of motherhood—me who longed to be a mother, who'd be a wonderful mother, whose life was shaped and molded to be the perfect fit for a child? Instead I was going to have to watch and pretend to be happy for someone who I was absolutely certain hadn't planned to have this baby. I was furious at their lack of responsibility. How were they going to support a child when they could barely support themselves? I knew Jose; his grandchild would want for nothing, even if he and I were unable to pay our bills to do it. And what if the marriage didn't work out after all? What was going to happen to this baby then? Why wasn't the Universe more logical?

"Penny thinks this will be good for you," Jose said. "You know? Maybe help you."

I blew a sardonic snort of air out of my nose and kept smiling. Could anyone really be more clueless? It was nice that she empathized with my situation and that she thought her baby might help, but I was here to tell her that it wouldn't. This was such a typical response from someone who'd had no trouble whatsoever getting pregnant. Infertility 101: Handing over your precious baby isn't going to give an infertile woman her baby fix and make her feel better. And I didn't need anyone's so-called help.

I felt my face harden into a mean grimace, the muscles in my cheeks twitching from the strain and my teeth pressing together so hard that my jaw quivered. I felt five years of frustration and unvoiced resentment swirling inside and bubbling up. I wanted to let it out. I wanted to voice every hateful, vengeful thought I'd ever had. I wanted to direct every ounce of venom at my stepdaughter for daring to have a baby when she knew full well I couldn't! I wanted to stomp off into a corner and refuse to have anything to do with this baby who would invade my misery and force me to face the cold fact that I would never be a mother. And I wanted to tell Jose every single word of what I was thinking. But when I glanced over at him, I saw his emotions painted clearly on his face, a tortured mixture of apology for having to give me the news, fear that I was going to finally explode, and the gentle glow of a man who was stepping gracefully, with his hair, teeth and pride intact, into a new role as Grandfather. So I bit my tongue. I bit it so hard it hurt. I wrapped my toes, one across the other, until they squashed against the hard curve of my hiking boots, and I kept telling stories about the Alps.

Back at home, I tossed my backpack onto the bed, and gave the cat a cursory scratch on the head. She nosed around while I built a small mountain of dirty socks and t-shirts on the floor, trying not to pitch them with too much attitude. I dug out the cowbell, the packet of Edelweiss seeds and the feathered Alpine hatpin I'd brought for Jose. I'd been so pleased with my purchases 7,000 miles ago, but compared to the news he'd just unloaded on me, they were trivial trinkets. For a fleeting moment I considered flinging them all in the trash, telling Jose I'd just brought myself as a gift, and demanding to know if that was enough. Then the cat pawed at the tissue paper wrapping around the hatpin and unfurled a curious claw. I scooped her up into my arms and rested my forehead on hers. I closed my eyes and breathed in the warm scent of her fur and the faint aroma of tuna. I hugged her, trying to calm my rage and slow my breathing, until she finally wriggled free.

This wasn't Jose's fault and I couldn't direct my hatred at him. This was a big life moment for him, a huge milestone, as his child became a parent. His family tree had extended down to the next generation, moving him up one step closer to that revered position of family patriarch, the role still held by his father. His parents would be great-grandparents; there would be four generations of his family living at once. It was an enormous landmark in his family's history, and it had nothing to do with me. My twig of the family tree had butted up against a brick wall, beyond which it would never extend, but his was still growing and would continue to grow and expand long after I had ceased to be an important link in anyone's genealogy research. In future generations, he would be the great-great-great-great grandfather; I would be the Weird Childless Aunt.

So, I stewed in my own bitter tea and wondered how I was ever going to make it through this terrible ordeal with my dignity intact. I wondered if Penny would decide she wasn't ready to be a mother and offer her baby to me instead. I speculated as to whether I'd accept it. Would it be weird to raise my stepdaughter's child? It would certainly be complicated. Finally, I dismissed the idea as just another desperate plot to get what I wanted the easy way.

For the next few days I sulked. I trudged around the house, shuffling along in my slippers, dragging my bag of misery behind me. I didn't bring up the subject of Penny's pregnancy with Jose, but I brought it up with everyone else I knew. I told my friends, unfolding the drama for maximum impact, and I got a thrill of validation at the shocked expressions on their faces. They rallied behind me, wailing in sympathy at the injustice of my situation. They beat their war drums, denouncing pregnant women the world over, but before long, I could no longer raise my voice along with them. I was rallying troops for a battle I knew I'd never march into. My anger and self-pity, though justified, were not logical and not helpful. This wasn't Jose's fault; it wasn't even Penny's fault. *News Flash, Lisa*, I thought. *Life goes on. You can choose to go on with it, or you can get off the ride.*

Jose had been tiptoeing around me, deftly avoiding the subject of babies. I hated watching him being on his best behavior; I hated that I had taken away his joy; I hated that the happy family we had planned was now as fragile as the spotted shell of a quail egg. One night at dinner, I broke the silence. "You're going to be a grandpa," I said, settling my throat into a relaxed state, so that the words could float out on a cheerful wave.

"And you're going to be a grandma," he replied. "What do you think about that?"

A grandma.

My stomach flipped. The irony, the ridiculousness of it all. I was going to be a 38-year-old grandmother. I could see people's faces as they did the math, pegged me as a teenage mother, and hung all their assumptions and prejudices on me. I thought about all the times I'd wanted to be different, wanted to shake up the status quo, and how I'd managed to get what I'd wished for again. But after a few days, the idea took root and slowly began to bud.

I'd been so wrapped up in my thoughts about motherhood that grandmotherhood had barely occurred to me. Technically, I'd be a step-grandma, no blood relation at all, but to this new child, I'd just be Grandma Lisa, or Granny Lisa, or perhaps I could insist on being called simply Grandmama. This child wouldn't care about bloodlines and genes, only about cuddles and comfortable laps, giant ice creams and trips to the zoo, only about whose face popped around the door whenever Grandma came to visit. I remembered my own grandmothers, their kind faces, their individual Grandma scents—roast meat and disinfectant for one, face powder and fudge for the other. I had loved my grandmas and relished my visits with them. And now I was going to be a grandma—the best grandma the world had ever seen. I was going to love this baby, my grandchild, bloodline or no. There was going to be a new baby in the family and that baby would look to me, Grandma Lisa, for life's basic needs. It would be my job to provide all the best books and to read stories. I'd be there to explain life's complex conundrums, such as whether butterflies have knees, or if there's such a place as Old Zealand. I'd provide comfort for scraped knees and awe at lost teeth. This baby would be my grandchild, blood connection or none, and I realized that, despite myself, I was falling in love.

But I also realized I was in a predicament. I was concerned about *my* new grandchild's health and was worried about whether Penny was taking proper care of herself. Was she eating right? Was she feeding *my* grandchild junk food? Had she given up smoking? I prayed she had given up smoking, but what if she hadn't? How could I step in and voice my opinion when I had no experience of motherhood? Added to that, I was in the uncomfortable position of being merely a stepmother—and not even a stepmother who'd had any input in her upbringing. I had a limited right to stick my nose into her business in the way an actual mother could.

I'd missed a vital part of my training for my progression to the senior generation. I should have been the wise young mother, experienced but with more current information than her own mother, willing to pass on what I'd learned—advice on morning sickness, strollers, and colic. And in a way, I was. I'd spent five years preparing to be a mother. I knew all the things a pregnant woman ought to be doing to take care of herself—more information than a doctor would give out on a general visit. I knew about the dangers of BPA from plastic bottles; I had solid arguments for and against the use of pacifiers, and could state the case for cloth versus disposable diapers and vice versa. For five years, my ears, eyes and mind had been tuned towards everything baby. I had sat quietly in conversations including other pregnant women and silently collected information on every aspect of pregnancy, childbirth, and child rearing.

But in those situations, I could never voice an opinion of my own, for fear I'd be greeted with, "You don't have kids; you wouldn't understand."

So, although I wanted the very best start in life for my grandchild-to-be, I knew from experience that my "motherly advice" would carry no weight. So I made a pact with myself, a cowardly option perhaps, but one best designed to protect my raw feelings. I would minimize my time with Penny for the duration of her pregnancy and when all else failed, I would keep my mouth shut. It was a dumb plan, but it was all I had.

Eventually, my plan fell apart. Jose's mother was sick and getting worse, so we visited her every week. Penny wanted to see her grandmother but not without her dad, so the family decided to gather, and like it or not, the family included me.

The night before I was supposed to see Penny, I had a strange dream about winning a backstroke swim race on dry land. It was so hard trying to backstroke without water, but I tried really hard and ended up taking first place. In my dream, the essayist, Anne Lamott contacted me about including a piece I'd written about becoming a grandmother in an anthology she was publishing. It was a strange dream and I woke up early with an overpowering sense of sadness. I lay in bed for a while, thinking about the dream and trying to figure out the reason for this sudden dark cloud. Backstroking on dry land seemed like the perfect summary of everything I'd been through in the past five years, flailing around, unable to see where I was going, fighting to do something that was impossible. And yet, in the dream, I'd won the race. But still I felt deeply and wholly sad.

Slowly, it occurred to me that this new chapter in Penny's life was the end of a chapter in mine. I was passing on to the next generation the responsibility of bringing children into the world. I'd had my shot and it didn't work out. So, now I was skipping the natural progression from child to mother and going straight to being a grandmother. I suddenly felt very old and exhausted, but still, I would pull myself out of bed and put on my game face. I would put on a smile and be a doting, excited grandmother-to-be—because I was all of those things, even though underneath, the mother-that-never-would-be was profoundly sad.

There were three-and-a-half generations gathered at my in-laws' house that afternoon—Jose's parents, his sister Yolanda, two pregnant women—Jose's niece, Teresa, and Penny—and their two respective bumps that would soon begin the fourth generation. Penny had dressed in a snug tank top that showed off the tiny pooch that my mother-in-law said looked as if she'd eaten too much spaghetti. Teresa, at seven months, looked as if she was about to pop any second. The men beat a hasty retreat into the backyard to smoke cigars and I took my place inside with the women. I was on my best behavior; I *oohed* and *aahed* as Penny passed around her ultrasound pictures, and I joked that the tiny almost indistinguishable peanut looked exactly like Jose. I was still laughing when Penny pulled out a pocket Doppler—a portable version of the kind used to listen to the baby's heartbeat—and maneuvered the wand over her smooth pale belly. I held my breath, listening to the static noise and trying to keep my own heart rate in check. And then I heard it, faint at first, but then more clear, the tiny flutter of a baby's heartbeat. It seemed so fragile and so fast, the sound of a little being, determined to stay alive and grow into somebody's baby. I felt my eyes sting with the threat of tears. I blinked them back down, willing my emotions under control. *Not today,* I thought. Today wasn't my day to feel sorry for myself. It wasn't my day for regrets or resentment. I had to be strong around these young women. I had to show them

I was happy for them and their futures. I needed them to know that they shouldn't be afraid to be happy around me, but all the same I wanted to cry for the heartbeat I would never get to hear.

I listened as Penny and Teresa relayed all the strange things they'd experienced with their new pregnant bodies. They were excited and a little bit scared, just as I knew I would have been, and I watched them make the transition into a new stage of their lives, and take on a new air of maturity. I was pleased to see it happening, but I sat in silence and listened. I stuck to my plan to keep my mouth shut and acted as if I had nothing to contribute. Even when the discussions turned to subjects on which I had knowledge or opinions, I bit my tongue. I'd read that it wasn't good for the baby to have too many unnecessary ultrasounds, such as the 4D ones they were planning to have multiple times. A friend's doctor had told her it was okay to drink a small amount of caffeine, suggesting it would cause less harm to the baby than a mother stressed out because she couldn't get her daily fix. But I didn't speak up; I was afraid of getting that look that said, "What do you know?" and I knew that today I wouldn't be able to stand it. Maybe someday I'd find value in my own knowledge and my own unique perspective, but not today.

Eventually, the conversation turned to names. Penny was certain she was having a boy and all the family voodoo confirmed it, although it was too soon for a doctor to verify. Consequently, she was unwilling to share her shortlist of boys' names, but as she wasn't planning to use them, she was happy to share the girls'.

"We like Sophia," she told us.

The sound of that name coming from her mouth was like a kick to the gut. Of all the beautiful names available, she had to pick that one. I'd withstood all the other tests of the day so far, but not this. This was my worst fear, that she'd unknowingly take away my baby's name. I wanted to stand up and yell that she couldn't use it. Sophia was *my* grandmother's name, not hers, and it was the name we had chosen for our little girl. I wanted to yell, "No!" but instead I said, "Who's hungry? I think I'll go to the store and get something to fix for dinner."

It wasn't until I was outside in the driveway that I realized I hadn't taken a complete breath for the last two hours, as if filling my lungs with air might push loose all the emotions I was trying so hard to keep in place. I just wanted to be on my own, to feel sorry for myself if I wanted to, to cry if I felt I had to; I didn't want to put on a brave face for anyone any more. If this was a test of my mettle, I was happy to just fail. I was tired of being strong, of saying it was okay when it wasn't okay, not at all okay. But I needed to be.

The thesaurus game I'd once played had turned up definitions for *infertile*, such as *idle, wasteful, futile,* and *pointless*. They had all seemed like perfect descriptions of me. But I wasn't really pointless. I wasn't really using up valuable oxygen that ought to be saved for a producing woman. I had value, even if I couldn't have children. Feeling sorry for myself and staying in bed for the next 30 years was certainly an option, but then I really *would* be wasteful, futile, and pointless. I had to pick myself up and move on. I had to find the point to my life, even if it was just to be able to leave my accumulated millions to my cat.

So, I went to the store and I bought lettuce and tomatoes and an overpriced but perfectly ripe avocado, and I drove back to the house to face my demons. I couldn't spend the rest of my life avoiding pregnant women, just because it wasn't fair that it wasn't me. In a few more months, these women would have babies and what would I do then? Refuse to hold them because they

made me think of the baby I couldn't have? Was I going
to be unkind to these women because they had what I
wanted? I decided I couldn't do that. I loved these
women and I would love their babies, too.

But I didn't love all women with babies. When I got
back from the store, armed with the ingredients to make
my salad, my sister-in-law's godchildren were back from
their grandmother's house. I'd been expecting their
arrival and had been looking forward to spending some
time with them. The children belonged to Tiffany, a
young woman who lived across the street. They had
been in Yolanda's custody on-and-off since their
mother's first stint in jail for a drug-related crime.
Whenever they were at Yolanda's house, I tried to spend
time with them. They were sweet kids who'd found
themselves in a bad situation.

I had been surprised when Yolanda had told me the
kids would be at the house that day. "I thought they
were going back to their mother again."

Yolanda's face curled up into a disgusted expression.
"Yeah, well five days before they were due to go
home, she was pulled over high on meth and with a
loaded gun in the glove box of her car, so they're staying
with me."

I wanted to be sick. We'd been taught in our
adoption classes to keep our opinions about the
biological parents to ourselves, but that didn't mean we
were barred from having those opinions—and I certainly
had one. I was furious with Tiffany for blowing her life
and totally disregarding the lives of her children. I
wondered what kind of mother kept a gun in the car
with two small children around, and what the hell was
she doing carrying a weapon anyway? Most of all, I
wondered what kind of higher power gave two beautiful
children to this woman, but denied me. Was there no
justice in this world?

The kids were tired when they arrived. Yolanda fed them supper and put them to bed, and I began to think about my own bed and my own peaceful home. As the evening came to a merciful end, Yolanda asked to borrow Penny's pocket Doppler for a few minutes. When she headed out the front door, I didn't need to ask where she was going. I knew she was going across the street to see Tiffany; it was the only place she could be going, and the only reason to take the pocket Doppler would be because the girl was pregnant again. I glanced at Teresa and gave her a questioning look. She grimaced and nodded. I closed my eyes and shook my head, no longer trying to make any sense of the world. When I opened them again, I caught the last snippet of a sentence as Teresa whispered something to Penny. The only thing I heard was, "twins."

There was no rhyme or reason to how the Universe divvied up its various blessings. There certainly wasn't any fairness to it. I couldn't imagine why the Universe, in its infinite wisdom, kept doling out chance after chance to this useless girl, and yet had singled me out for childlessness. I was intelligent and came from a good, kind, and relatively normal family. I thought things through, was conscious of my actions, and would raise a child thoughtfully, with the aim of creating a good human being. I wouldn't do drugs, carry guns, or leave someone else the responsibility for my children. I deserved to be a mother, damn it! And yet, the Universe granted children to people who didn't deserve them, who wouldn't do a good job of raising them. Where was the justice in that?

Some people believe that the Universe only gives a person as much as she can handle. This argument is used to justify why good, kind people suffer terrible illnesses or impossible issues with family members. So, was the Universe trying to tell me that I wasn't up to motherhood? Looking around the room I knew I was just as capable and as ready as any of the other mothers-to-be. So maybe the Universe had decided instead that I was strong enough to handle the blow of childlessness. Perhaps it trusted me to stay calm and answer appropriately every time someone asked, "So, when are you guys going to have kids?" Perhaps it thought that a book-smart mother who could look at situations objectively and offer coolheaded advice to her friends was what I was better equipped to do. Maybe I was destined for some great adventure that could never have been made with kids in tow. I appreciated the Universe's vote of confidence in me, but I didn't want to pass its test.

14
I Can Quit Anytime

During my spring-cleaning that year I came across the notebook in which Jose and I had once compiled a list of places we wanted to visit and things we wanted to do. Not much had been checked off in recent years and Mount Everest Base Camp, the Taj Mahal and surfing in South Africa were still waiting for us. Our travel budget had been eaten up by medical expenses, and our general health and increased weight meant that trekking to 17,000 feet was out of the question, but more than that, we no longer had the heart to plan an adventure or the stamina to step away from the safety of our small circle of existence.

We were tired. We had lived nothing-but-baby for almost five years and somewhere along the way, we had lost ourselves. We had lost the strength to try new things and could no longer remember what it was we had once loved. But it was time to rekindle our dreams and time to work on falling in love again. We were coming to terms with the idea that we would never have children together. I was reassessing myself as a woman without children and even looking forward to my new role as grandmother. We had to remember why we'd first fallen in love, and in a way, we had to start over, rebuilding our relationship on this new foundation of a family without children.

"If I can't have kids," I said to Jose one day, "then I just want to travel." I thought he'd be pleased to see I was on the road to recovery, but for a brief instant I saw a look of pain run across his eyes. I couldn't let it get to me. I had to stay the course and focus on moving on, so I updated our list of travel destinations and made a pledge to start checking things off soon.

First on our list was Jose's wish to see the Moa on Easter Island, and we'd discovered that we could get there via Santiago, Chile, or Tahiti. There was no contest. We'd seen Santiago (for a day, at least) and Tahiti sounded like the perfect place for a second honeymoon, a chance to rest, put the frustrations of the last few years behind us, and remember why it was we had fallen in love in the first place. I went to the bookstore to look for a travel guide.

The travel books were on the row of shelves near the cookbooks, which ran back-to-back with the books on health. Although I had no intention of even looking there, before I knew it I was standing in the Infertility section holding the *Lonely Planet Guide to French Polynesia* and a book about fertility and Chinese medicine. It was an old habit, searching books for something new, that magic elixir that might hold the key to my fertility. I'd been doing it for so long that it felt comfortable.

I flipped to the Contents page of the fertility book, but hesitated. We were supposed to be coming to terms with the idea of not having children, and trying to piece our lives together again. This book wouldn't help that. But I was curious. I didn't expect it to tell me anything I hadn't already read a hundred times, but I wanted to see what these authors had to say, what gave them the right to write another damn book on curing infertility. And I wanted to see if maybe there was some gem of information that I'd overlooked, something that might offer the key to motherhood for me.

I found a seat in a quiet corner of the store and scanned the author bios. One was Doctor Yen, a practitioner of traditional Chinese medicine, and the other was one of his miracle patients. A doctor-patient team; that was new. I sat for an hour, reading case histories of women with severe fertility issues who had been to see this Doctor Yen. Every one had a success story. I felt my pulse quicken. I flicked through the chapters until I found the story of a woman who had only a portion of one ovary. She was an impossible case and had been told she would never be able to get pregnant. Her story was infinitely more hopeless than mine. I flipped over one page and then the next, scanning the story for the information I dared not hope to see, but knew would be there.

I took a pregnancy test—and it came back positive!
I read on, looking to see what happened next.
When my daughter was born...
I stared at the words, *my daughter,* and all the brave words I'd spoken about being okay and about accepting the hand I'd been dealt, fluttered away as if caught up on a sudden gust of wind. For all my talk, I wasn't okay. I wanted to be a success story, too; I still wanted *my* miracle. And I knew that my talk of recovery and coming to terms, of moving on, was all just a façade, a good show I put on for the crowd.

I flicked to the back of the book and discovered that the doctor's clinic was less than 20 miles from my home.
But you've tried Chinese medicine before, said my voice of reason.
"Yes," I said, "but this is different. This man could

really help me."

But you said you were done with all that.

"I know," I said. "But I lied."

What about Jose?

"Shut up," I told the voice. "Nobody asked you."

I bought the book, took it home and put it on the bottom shelf of my office bookcase, with the spine facing in. I didn't want Jose to see it, not yet. If I'd lied to myself, I'd lied to him, too, and I wasn't ready to admit that to him yet. But more than that, I was afraid he wouldn't back me up this time and I wasn't ready to face that.

Every day, before Jose got home from work, I read a little bit of the book. I read about nutrition, meditation, acupuncture, and herbs—all the things I'd read before— but there was something in Doctor Yen's words that wafted a gentle breeze over the embers of hope that I hadn't realized were still glowing inside me. And when I heard Jose at the front door, I hid the book again and went out to greet him with a smile. It didn't occur to me that this was the behavior of an addict, hiding my habit from my loved ones, but that's exactly what it was. I was addicted to solving the puzzle of my infertility. And just like an addict crying for help, eventually I left the evidence out for Jose to find.

Jose mentioned the book just once and asked me casually why I was reading it.

"Just curious," I said, and he didn't press me any further.

One night after dinner, Jose was washing dishes while I put away the leftovers. I scraped rice from the rice cooker into a Tupperware, dusting the stray grains off the counter into my hand and into the trash, with a practiced flick of my wrist. I watched as Jose unscrewed the top of his Italian coffee percolator and tapped the used coffee grounds into the ceramic compost jar beside the sink. He didn't look like the man I had fallen in love with; he just looked like the man who shared my house. There was no glow to his face, and I felt no tingle of excitement in mine. We were two people coexisting, living under the same roof, but divided by a secret.

I took a cloth, dipped it into the hot water and began to wipe down the tile counter tops. "So, I've been thinking about something and I wanted to tell you about it," I said, not looking over at Jose, but sensing him watching me.

"What's that?" he said.

"Well, I found this book about Chinese Medicine...."

"The fertility book."

I nodded, avoiding his eyes. "U-huh."

"Do you want to go and see him? The doctor?" said Jose.

I stopped wiping, just for a second, caught off-guard that Jose seemed to have known this was coming. "Kind of," I said.

"Then you should go."

I glanced at him, trying to read his expression to guess the motivation behind this cool acceptance. I saw resignation, and I knew that now he was doing this simply to keep me happy. But it didn't matter. I'd been looking for a "yes" vote, and he'd given it to me without question. "Let's just give it three months," I told him. "Just three months and then I'll stop. At least that way I'll know I tried everything and then I'll be able to walk away."

"Will you?" he said.

I squared my shoulders. "Absolutely."

For the next three months I drove an hour each way, twice a week to see Doctor Yen. I was absolutely determined to be another one of his success stories; maybe I'd even make it into his next book. I wanted a baby, I wanted to find the solution, and I didn't want to have to find out whether I could keep my word to Jose. Doctor Yen was wonderful. He had a gentle spirit and a calm persona, just as advertised in his book, but when it came to solving the puzzle of me, he was a pit bull. I followed his directions to the letter, searching the Asian markets for quail eggs and sea cucumbers, and stocking my pantry with goji berries and raspberry leaf tea. I made pots of herbal infusions that filled the kitchen with the scent of rotting leaves, but I drank the tea religiously, ate the foods he suggested, exercised, and even meditated. I felt a great hope that Doctor Yen could help me, and when I saw pregnant women in his waiting room, I wondered how their situations compared to mine, if they had given up, and if Doctor Yen had saved them, too.

Every time we met, Doctor Yen reviewed every detail in my chart, flipping pages back and forth, asking questions, and calculating his next prescription. "You're very tricky to figure out," he'd say. "Let's try something else." I always agreed. I knew that if anyone could figure out how to fix me, he could. So when my three months was up, I made another series of appointments. "I feel like I'm so close," I told Jose. "I can't stop now."

Jose always asked how my appointments had gone and I filled him in on the latest line of thought. "You should come too," I told him. "He's really great."

But Jose refused. He went through the motions for me, resumed our routine of tracking my cycle and calendaring sex, but I could tell his heart wasn't in it. I needed him to do everything he could to make this work this time, but I didn't have the energy to help him.

Doctor Yen never gave up on me. He had the utmost faith that he could help me and so I had the utmost faith in him. Even when I was frustrated, he never stopped believing

"I don't get it," I snapped one day. "Why isn't it working?"

Doctor Yen didn't take offense at my outburst. He took my hand and said in his calm gentle voice. "It *is* working. Your body is just resisting and we have to be patient."

I didn't want to be patient any more. I'd been patient for almost five years and I needed this to work. I'd promised Jose I would stop after this, but we both knew that was a lie. I'd uncover some other piece of information, another magic elixir, and then I'd just try that, then just try something else. This would never end. Not until I got what I wanted.

Doctor Yen squeezed my hand again and smiled in his soothing, nurturing way. "I know it's frustrating, but it will all be worth it when you get your baby."

I nodded, but in my mind I heard myself say, "Forget the stupid baby, just figure out why this isn't working."

On the drive home, I thought about my reaction. This whole game was no longer about having a baby, or even about getting pregnant. All I wanted was to solve the puzzle. I wanted to figure out the why. Why were my ovaries misbehaving? Why wasn't Doctor Yen's treatment working? Why had my body let me down? I'd reconciled the fact that I could live without children, that I'd be okay if I never became a mother, but I couldn't reconcile the fact that my body had failed. I'd entered into a race for motherhood and all I really wanted was to win.

About five months into my treatment, Doctor Yen pored over my charts one day and shook his head. "Your body is stubborn," he said.

"Just like the rest of me," I quipped, trying to make light of an obvious and extremely frustrating situation.

"It just doesn't want to do this."

Well, make it, I thought, as I lay down on the table for Doctor Yen to place the acupuncture needles in my body.

I lay there in the semidarkness of the room, trying to

take deep breaths, trying to assuage my growing frustration and irritability. So my body didn't want to do this. What was that supposed to mean? My body didn't have control over me; I was in control over *it*. And Doctor Yen could make my body do as it was told. So what if my body didn't want to do this? I was going to make it.

I thought back to Doctor Hassan, the fertility doctor we'd first seen, what felt like a lifetime ago now. He had wanted to force my body to do what it didn't want to do. He had wanted to force it with drugs and procedures. I had refused to do that, not willing to pay the consequences of meddling with nature. Now Doctor Yen was trying to force it with herbs and needles, but nothing had changed. My body didn't want to produce a baby.

I had been such a good liar, I'd even fooled myself. But the truth hit me full on now. My infertility had nothing to do with Karma. I hadn't done something wicked in a past life that made me unworthy of being a mother in this one. My situation had nothing to do with destiny, or fate, or bad luck. There was no higher power controlling my future for reasons that I could not yet see. These were all excuses I'd fabricated to explain a fact I wasn't prepared to face. There was something wrong with my body and it knew it shouldn't reproduce, plain and simple. Science and evolution were hard at work, ensuring the survival of the fittest and there was something in my genetic makeup, something in my body that was not strong enough to be replicated. The future of the human race was not me. There was a reason my body didn't want to create a baby. I didn't know the reason, but I knew I had to listen to my body; I had to let go of my pigheadedness, and I had to let go of my dream.

The following week I skipped one of my

appointments with Doctor Yen and the week after that I skipped both. The week after that, Jose noticed and asked what was going on. I couldn't look him in the eye when I told him about Doctor Yen's analysis of my body's refusal to budge, but when I glanced up, the pained look on his face told me he had reached the same conclusion. Finally, this was where it would all end. This was where it *had* to end.

Jose and I tiptoed around one another for a week or two. We didn't talk about what had happened or about the consequences of our decision. I knew he would ask me if I was okay and I would tell him I was. But I wasn't. I whirled through the stages of grief all over again, angry that this had happened, then denying that it was possible, and depressed when I faced the reality that it was. I had long since run out of bargaining chips and I had no interest in acceptance. Somewhere in my gut I knew that stopping was the right decision, but it didn't stop it from feeling wrong. So I avoided the subject and so did Jose.

Eventually, though it became like a dead moose in the middle of the room; there was no way we could avoid it and it was beginning to stink.

"So what now?" Jose said finally.

I shrugged. I'd reconciled what wasn't to be, but I didn't know what was next.

"Back to adoption?" he said.

"You don't want to do that," I said.

He looked away and I knew I shouldn't have said that. "I won't lie to you," he said. "I'm afraid we're going to get our hearts broken."

I *knew* we would, but wouldn't it be worth it?

"I'm not sure mine will stand up to it again," he said.

I felt myself recoil at his honesty. We had tried to have a baby for five years and neither of us had the emotional stamina to set out on another long and treacherous journey. The social worker had told us that adoption wasn't for the faint of heart and our hearts were practically unconscious. But this was our last ray of hope, and if Jose couldn't find the strength to go on, that last ray would be snuffed out.

I was in a no-win situation. If we moved ahead with adoption, we would get our hearts broken, somewhere along the line, and I didn't want to subject Jose to that. But if we didn't move forward, I would never be a mother and that wouldn't be fair to me. I felt trapped between caring for Jose and caring for my own needs and wants.

Jose let out a deep exhale. "I'll do it," he said, "but I want to use a different agency."

"What?" I said. "If we do that we'll have to start all over again."

Jose stood firm. "I don't want to go through that agency," he said. "They're not competent."

I felt a growl brewing in the back of my throat. "This has nothing to do with incompetence," I said. "You just don't like Nadine."

"No," he said. "I don't *trust* her."

He was being stubborn and making a point of being difficult, but I didn't want to start that fight; I didn't have the strength to finish it. "Then who *do* you want to use?" I almost spat the words at him.

"The place downtown."

"That's all the way *past* downtown. It's too far," I told Jose again, reinforcing that it would take us well over an hour to make the drive to class.

"It's just for six weeks. It's worth it to work with a good agency."

"But it's not just six weeks, is it?" I said, feeling the heat rise in my face as all the frustration I'd been holding in started rising to the surface. "Because then there'll be follow-up visits and there'll be visitations with the birth parents, and you won't be the one schlepping the poor kid to Downtown L.A. and back three times a week!"

"That's what people with kids do. You're not going to have time to yourself anymore. You just do what you need to do for the kids."

"I know that," I said. "I understand. But why go into it already making it harder than it needs to be?"

We glared at each other for a moment and then he said, "Fine. We'll do it your way."

His words reverberated, as if they'd been a hard slap. I didn't think I was being unreasonable or demanding. It made sense to use a closer agency. And now Jose was being petulant. He was making this much more difficult than it needed to be. It was as if he didn't really want to do this.

And then it dawned on me: he didn't. It was so obvious I don't know why I hadn't seen it before. Jose was exhausted. He'd been trying for so long to get me my baby and it was clear he didn't want to do it any more. He was five years older than when we'd first begun our quest. Whether we adopted a child or had a miracle baby, he would be in his 70s before our child made it to college. Assuming Jose lived that long. He'd done his stint, doing what he had to do for me, but now he had a granddaughter coming and it was clear to me; Jose no longer wanted children with me.

That evening, sitting on the opposite side of the living room from Jose, each of us pulling the edges of our separate worlds closer around ourselves, I made a decision.

I'll do it without him, I thought. *I'll just wait until he's dead, and then I'll adopt a child by myself.*

It was too hard to keep fighting for what I wanted when he kept dragging me down. He was the only man I'd ever trusted to father my children, but now he was turning against me. We'd been a great team once, but now we were on opposing sides. So, I started to calculate how long my husband might have to live and what terrible fate might befall him. I started counting down the days I'd have to wait.

And when he was gone, I'd finally get the child I wanted.

15
Choices

Driving up Interstate 5 once, Jose and I had followed for several miles behind a large SUV. Through the back window I could see the bright glow of two small video screens and the soft, top corner of a child's safety seat. The screens were showing different movies, both with bright cartoon images flashing in rapid succession. "What a shame," I had thought.

As a child, I had loved road trips around my native Britain. I loved traveling through new territory, taking in the sights and seeing things I'd never seen before. I can remember seeing my first wind turbine, mounted on a tall thin tower at the peak of a hill and wondering what it was and what it did. I saw vast fields of bright yellow flowers, farmers' cover crops, and thinking how pretty they looked. I saw giant red combined harvesters, gathering and bundling tall sheaves of wheat. I saw shaggy Highland cattle with their long red coats and wide horns. I traveled over the wild tangle of highway transitions at Birmingham's Spaghetti Junction, through a mile-long tunnel running underneath the River Tyne, and across the Humber Bridge, at the time, the world's longest single span suspension bridge. There was so much to see beyond my little suburban neighborhood and I always returned home with new experiences and new information about the world in which I lived.

Interstate 5 runs the full length of the Western States from the Mexico border all the way into British Columbia. Even on the stretch through Central California, where there appears to be nothing but the boring flat plain of the San Joaquin Valley, there's so much to see and so many new things to discover. There's the chance to see where your produce comes from as you pass through the patchwork fields of grapes, oranges, pistachios and vegetables of California's agricultural center. You can see Harris Ranch, a sprawling (stinking) cattle farm, proof that hamburgers weren't always round. I-5 runs generally parallel to the California Aqueduct and the San Andreas Fault, ripe opportunities to learn about the source of Los Angeles Water and the reason for all the earthquakes. At various places the highway intersects Highway 198, the gateway to the Giant Sequoia National Monument, Highway 46, where James Dean was killed in his Porsche Spyder, and Highway 152, the road to Gilroy, the self-proclaimed garlic capital of the world. There's so much to see, so many chances to learn something new, ask a million questions, and maybe even get some answers. It seemed a shame that the children in the SUV, glued to their cartoons, missed all this. For them, it was all about what happened at the end—the vacation in the mountains, the weekend in San Francisco, or the holidays with Grandma. That journey was all about the destination.

I was no different from those children, except that my destination was motherhood. Five years earlier I had strapped myself in and set my sights on the end result— a baby. And while I'd been driving towards my goals, my life—the good life I already had—had been passing me by. At various times during my trip I had passed up opportunities because I wanted to have a baby. I gave up the sports I loved—running, biking, ocean swimming—for fear I might overtax my body and make it inhospitable for new life. I passed up the chance to try new activities—Cyclo cross, rock climbing, trapeze classes—because they might be dangerous if I was pregnant. I put off making trips to places I wanted to visit, on the off-chance I might suddenly become pregnant. I was afraid to go to Guatemala to see Antigua and the pyramids of Tikal, not because I'd heard stories of kidnapped tourists and malarial mosquitoes, but because I was afraid I might get food poisoning or heat exhaustion, and harm my nonexistent baby. For five years I hadn't done anything that needed to be planned more than six weeks in advance, just in case the next cycle was the one when I got pregnant. And I'd be just the same if I had children—giving up everything for them.

It was imagining Jose's eulogy that brought me to my senses. I thought back to when we'd met, the wonderful friendship that had bloomed, and that moment, when I'd been in Austria, halfway around the world from him, that I'd realized how much I wanted to be with him. I was going to miss his smile, miss his laughter when I said something smart. I was going to miss the walks along the beach to dinner. I was going to miss exploring new cities with him. Most of all, I was going to miss our conversations. I was going to miss him coming home from work with something he'd heard on the radio and striking up a discussion, or sometimes a serious debate, about the arguments for and against the draft, the benefits of recycling, or which country produced the best chocolate. When I tried to imagine my life without him in it, I felt hollow and cold.

I had been 32-years-old before I'd finally found someone I knew I wanted to spend my life with. Jose had been more than just a good-looking, fun-loving guy; he'd been more than a nice guy, or even a big adventure. Although he had been all those things, he had been my friend first, and a good friend at that. He had taught me how to appreciate art, fine wine, and The Three Stooges. He'd introduced me to low-rider cars, Catholic Saints, and Los Lobos, and sparked my interest in politics, opera, and stinky cheese. In return, I'd been responsible for getting him his first passport, and taking him to three new continents, ten new countries, and countless cities he'd never seen before. I'd introduced a city boy to the great outdoors, and nurtured in him a love of gardening and British comedy. He'd supported my desire to write and facilitated my transition from corporate drone to freelance writer. I'd encouraged him to go back to school and get a degree to teach history. We were good for each other. Living with him was never a battle for power. We were a team, and together, the whole was better than the sum of the parts—and the parts weren't bad to begin with. Jose had been the reason I had started the motherhood journey and I didn't want to do it without him.

Thankfully, he wasn't dead yet. But imagining life without him made me realize how much I wanted to get on with my life *with* him.

We didn't have a family pow-wow about our decision to not have children. I didn't make a chart listing the pros and cons of either lifestyle, assigning points and selecting the most advantageous option. We just stopped talking about it. When my prenatal vitamins ran out, I switched to a brand designed for women over 40. One day I tossed out all my fertility supplements and another day I added Doctor Yen's herbs to my compost pile, sending them literally back to the earth. Another day I added my friend's maternity top, my *Meditation for Fertility* CDs, and six pairs of baby socks to the Goodwill box. Bit by bit, I let go of my dream of motherhood.

The subject of our having children eventually came up in conversation and Jose opted not to let it pass. "We haven't talked about us and our plans for while," he said.

"There are no plans," I said, without a hint of bitterness.

"So we're done?" he asked.

I nodded.

He considered me for a few moments, maybe searching my face for signs of a lie. "Are you okay with that?"

"Yes," I said. "I am. Are you?"

He didn't answer, but I saw his head nod, just a brief movement, and then one side of his mouth curled up into the barest hint of a smile and I knew that my husband and I would have a good life together.

So I chose to end my quest for motherhood and live for the now. I believed that, given time, Doctor Yen could have made my body do what I wanted; Doctor Hassan could have implanted sufficient eggs that one or two would have made it; Doctor Forester could have eased us through the process of finding an egg donor; and the adoption agency could have matched us with a child in need of a loving home. Maybe my body would have had some weird hormonal surge and produced a viable egg just around the time Jose and I were making love, just for fun. I wouldn't be the first peri-menopausal woman to get such a surprise, and I certainly wouldn't be the oldest. Maybe it would still happen. Maybe I'd still get to be a mother—someday, somehow—and I'd be a good and devoted mother, and glad for the chance. I'd always wanted to be a mother, and that hadn't changed, but I could no longer sacrifice my life for something that might never be. The price was too high.

On the line was my relationship with Jose, my sanity, and my long-ago-lost sense of humor. If I quit now, I'd be free from the craziness and have the chance of a brand-new start with Jose. Yes, I'd give up the chance of motherhood, the unconditional love, acceptance in society and my place in the family. I'd have to admit that I had failed. But my single-minded drive for motherhood had to end, because I had a life to live, with Jose, and I had to get on with it, before it was too late.

Jose and I were already a family—a small family of two people, one cat, and a fish—but we were a family all the same. I had worried what my future would be like without children, but the future is always unknown. All we really have for sure is the now and my now was pretty good. It was time to start a new chapter.

16
Rebirth

Year 6

Mason Angela was born on a drizzly morning in February and she was beautiful. She had her father's pale skin, blue eyes, and a fuzz of reddish-blonde hair, but I announced loyally that she looked just like her mother. I waited patiently while her blood grandmother, Jose's ex-wife, held her granddaughter for the first time. I felt my heart quavering in my chest and I urged it to beat steady. When it was my turn, I took Mason gently in my arms and held her close to me. I felt the warmth of her skin and the faint smell of fresh new baby. I examined her almost invisible eyebrows and feathery eyelashes, her tiny velvet ear that had been folded over for eight-and-a-half months, and her delicate pink fingers tipped with impossibly small dots of fingernail. And I didn't wish she were mine.

I whispered to her gently, so that only she could hear, and I explained that I was her Grandma and told her all about the wonderful adventures she was going to have. I held her for as long as I could before conceding that I had to share and then I passed her to her Grandpa. For a few seconds, Grandpa Jose looked terrified that he'd been given such a valuable package to care for, but then he pushed his glasses up onto his head and smiled at his granddaughter. I had never seen such love in his eyes. The tiredness from the long morning's wait melted away and he smiled down at her. "Hello," he said. "It's very nice to meet you." I smiled and my heart filled with love for him. It would have been wonderful having children with him, and now it was going to be wonderful being grandparents.

When Travis took his daughter back, I saw a man I'd never seen before. The boy I'd worried wasn't ready to be a father, glowed with pride, held his baby girl like an old pro and talked to her as if they'd known one another for a lifetime. He was a proud father and suddenly a responsible husband; it looked as if the new family would be just fine.

At first Penny seemed uncertain about taking care of her baby, afraid perhaps of doing it wrong, but I could see that once she got the hang of it, she was going to be a good and pragmatic mother. As I watched her step into motherhood, I felt a twinge of sadness. I had a strange sensation, perching nervously in the hospital chair, watching Penny tend to her new daughter. I felt as if I were in an old black-and-white movie, standing on the end of a railway station platform, watching the 10:30 train pull away. It was a train I wanted to catch, and just like in those great romantic movies, I ran alongside the carriages, desperate to get onboard. But finally the platform ended and all I could do was watch the train pull away with motherhood onboard. All I could do was give a little wave and call out, "Write to me when you get there!" I was standing on the deserted platform, the dry leaves blowing around my feet and the porter walking by, whistling a long forgotten love song. "I'm afraid that was the last train, Miss," he'd say, and I would know that it was time for me to go home.

On Memorial Day weekend, Jose and I made plans for our three days off. We had decided to "go to Greece" for the weekend, not physically, but we would turn off our phones and pretend we were out of town, go to the beach and have dinner at a well-known local Greek restaurant, where there would be music and dancing. It would be a way to break our cycle of monotony and begin the process of being a couple again. The closer the weekend got, the more we were excited about the idea of our "stay-cation."

After dinner on Saturday, when our bellies were full of flamed cheese and roast lamb and I'd been softened by a vat of Greek wine, Jose said, a little sheepishly, "I know it's not in Greece, but I'd like to go to the cemetery to put flowers on my grandparents' graves. Will you come with me?"

I said I would.

When Jose's mother had passed away the previous November, she'd left strict instructions regarding her final wishes. There was to be no hoopla, no elaborate funeral, no weepy memorial service, and certainly no religious marker in the Catholic cemetery where her siblings and parents were buried. She was to be cremated and her ashes sprinkled around the roses in her garden. Her wishes had been granted, but the people left behind had been unable to mourn her departure. Jose had stepped up to his role of helping his dad and sister through their loss, and dealing with the bureaucratic details of someone's passing, but he hadn't yet dealt with his own loss. Because there had been no ceremony, his mother had simply disappeared. He had held her hand one day and the next there had been a phone call saying that she was gone, and that was that. But in her efforts to protect her family from grief, she had unwittingly denied them the gift of closure.

Several months later I heard Jose crawl out of bed in the middle of the night and not come back. He sat out on the front porch and wept, finally able to acknowledge that she was gone, but he still had nowhere to leave his grief. He spent hours tracking down lost relatives and their gravesites, and began making weekly pilgrimages to place flowers on their graves. He never told me he was going, but I'd find discarded flower wrappers in the backseat of the car, so I knew that's where he'd been.

On the Monday morning of Memorial Day, I packed up a bag with a bowl, some dish soap and a sponge, a set of garden clippers, a trowel, and some scissors. As a child, I'd visited my grandparents' grave with my dad and aunts and watched their ritual of trimming the grass and cleaning the headstone. I understood later that it was the only way they knew how to keep caring for their parents after they were gone; it was the outlet for the love that was left behind.

It was a warm day and we made the half-hour drive to Calvary Cemetery in East L.A., an area of Los Angeles I seldom visited. We followed the map Jose had printed and stepped carefully over the rows of headstones set flush into the grass, until we found the grave of Victoria, his grandmother, whom he had loved so much. I set to work clipping the relentless crabgrass that had overgrown the edges of the stone and threatened to overrun the entire cemetery. I worked diligently and in silence, leaving Jose to his thoughts. The only thing I knew to do was to clean and maintain, my way of letting him know that I cared about his family, even the people I had never met. When I was finished, Jose placed a simple bouquet of flowers on the grave and we stood for a moment, at the crest of the hill, the roar of two intersecting freeways just a faint hum in the distance and the grey and grime of L.A.'s industrial area hidden behind the cover of an avenue of Valley Oaks. I wrapped my arms around Jose's shoulders and pulled him towards me. I felt his arms encircle my waist and his cheek rest on my shoulder.

"Thank you," he said.

"For what?"

"For taking care of my family."

By the time we had visited the graves of his grandfather, a great aunt, and three uncles, Jose's somber mood had lifted. The visit had satisfied his need to mourn his mother through her relatives and he was ready to embark on some more detective work. In the course of sifting through his mother's paperwork, he had come across burial sites for some other relatives and he wanted to find their graves. There was his mother's great aunt, who had never married but was rumored to have been buried holding a framed photo of her lost love, a soldier killed in the Civil War. Jose had also come across a receipt for the internment of a baby. The baby was listed as the child of one uncle, but the burial had been paid for by another. Jose had never heard about this baby, and we were both excited to solve the riddle and perhaps uncover some juicy family gossip.

The clerks at the office by the cemetery gates were just as excited and seemed to take great pride in solving mysteries and locating graves with the minimum of information. The great aunt's grave was easy to find and the clerk gave us a map showing the location, explaining that the grave had no marker, but there were landmarks—a faucet and a curb marking—that would help us pinpoint the spot. The baby's records were harder to find as we had little information to go on. Finally, the clerk came across a possibility. "Would the baby be Valentino?" she asked.

Jose nodded. "Quite possibly, if he was named after his father."

I flinched and pushed away the memory that we had planned to name our Valentino in honor of the same uncle. I pretended not to feel the tightening in my gut, but I gripped the little map and drove with Jose to the older part of the cemetery, closer to the front gates.

The clerk had explained that this grave would be hard to find, because it was also unmarked and located in a section where the graves were not in easily identifiable rows. We climbed the hill and I counted the rows as best I could, veering off at a slight angle away from Jose. Near the crest of the hill, the rows of headstones ended and I stepped into an area of tiny headstones, scattered almost randomly in a long triangle. I looked for numbers on the stones, trying to locate our site, and glanced at some of the inscriptions. *Our angel,* one said. One had dates just a few months apart; another had only one date, the date of birth and death. One even had a tiny faded photograph set into the stone. They all signified lives that had never had chance to begin and I gritted my teeth and tried not to imagine the baby I had never had.

I was reading an inscription when Jose signaled to me that he had found the grave of his baby cousin. I hurried over, stepping carefully between the stones, and stood by Jose, looking down at the bare patch of grass. There was no stone marker, nothing to show that baby Valentino had ever existed, no indication that he had once been cared for and loved.

As I stood there, I felt a strong current of cold emotion sweep up the hill, whipping over the gravestones, around my feet and up my body until it hit me full in the chest. I was overcome with the heavy dark feeling of loss, the loss of *my* Valentino, the baby who had never even been given the chance to exist, except in my imagination. There he had been real, with his black mop of hair, his dark almond eyes, and the mischievous smile that he got straight from his daddy. For five years I had envisioned him as the helpless baby, asleep on my chest, the laughing toddler testing out his legs, and the grown man I'd hoped he would become. But none of that had ever had the chance to be.

The weight of my loss pressed against my chest and for a moment I stopped breathing and my whole body was still. Just as Jose had been unable to gain closure for his mother's death, so had I been unable to bring finality to my own journey. There had been no ceremony to mark the passing of my motherhood, no announcement in the local newspaper, and no cards of sympathy from well-wishers. Concerned friends and neighbors hadn't rallied around, bringing casseroles and offering assistance, because my loss was not visible. There were no framed photos on the mantelpiece to show what had been taken away from me, and no ritual outlet for my grief. Infertility was a silent, unspoken loss, and I had not been given the chance to mourn.

I stepped away from the grave and allowed gentle tears of relief to flow down my cheeks. This part of our journey was over now and I was going to be okay. I could lay my desire for motherhood to rest now, mourn its passing, and move on with my life. I was safe now— no more doctors, no more needles, and no more frustrated attempts at pregnancy. Jose and I, our family of two, could get on with our lives now.

I knew there'd be times when the ghost of that desire would haunt me, when something would jostle my memories of what might have been and set me wondering "what-if" again. Perhaps one night I'd nestle into the couch with Jose and a bowl of popcorn and we'd settle in for three hours of *Gone With the Wind* and as Scarlet fled Atlanta I'd see Miss Melly look at her new baby with unconditional love, and I'd think, *I want to do that*. Or I'd go to a local Earth Day fair and see a great kid-friendly display of local snakes and frogs and think, *I wish I had a child that I could share this with.* Or a stranger on a plane would ask me to hold her baby and when she'd ask if I had kids of my own I'd forget to say, "No," and instead sigh wistfully and say, "Someday."

And that would be okay. It would be a reminder that I was human, that I have desires and that sometimes those desires remain unfulfilled. And I'd remember that I could still be a mother if I chose to be. I'd know that there were myriad avenues of reproductive medicine that we had chosen not to explore. There was adoption, domestic or foreign, private or through the Child and Family Services program. But I'd remember why I'd chosen not to take those paths. And that would be okay. And perhaps I'd think, *I'm not going to chase that miracle anymore...but maybe the miracle will find us anyway.* And that would be okay, too.

And for the times when it wasn't okay, I'd found a place to come, a place that could be just for me and my baby-that-never-was. An unmarked grave where I could come and sit and remember for a while. And then I could go on with my life, stride out into the world and see what it has to offer next.

I wiped my cheeks, took a deep breath and went back to Jose.

"You okay?" he said.

I nodded. "Yes."

"I'm sorry," he said. "I didn't mean for this to upset you."

"It's okay," I said. "It's good for me."

I took his hand and we walked silently down the hill and back to the car.

"You must be hungry," he said as I climbed into the driver's seat and pulled the car away from the curb.

"I am."

He smiled. "Are you feeling adventurous?"

The tone in his voice caused me to glance at him and I saw that familiar sly twinkle in his eye. My heart fluttered. "Okay," I said. "I'm game."

"Good," he said. "Let's go to King Taco."

I giggled like a silly lovesick teen and pointed the car towards the cemetery gates.

Acknowledgements

Sometimes it can seem like an endless road from "I have this idea" to "I have this book," but I've been fortunate to meet many good Samaritans along the way.

Barbara Abercrombie nudged me from student to published writer with care and class; Amy Friedman tricked me into writing about the one thing I didn't want to write about, and then encouraged me to keep going; and Jennie Nash put up with my whining and teeth gnashing until I'd rewritten every single word to the best of my ability.

Every day I'm grateful to The Sisters of Submission who coax, encourage, critique, and sometimes roll their eyes at my work. Shannon Calder, Roberta Wax, Jeff Buppert, and Kathleen Guthrie have read every single word *ad nauseum* and I thank them for their patience and encouragement. Thank you to Carollynn Bartosh for her friendship and support, to my dear friends Janeen Arrigo, Cheryl Lucero, and Stephanie Rausch for believing, and to my wonderful family for being as close to normal as anyone could wish.

This book looks beautiful due to the creative genius of Julia Clarke at ScarletHare, who was there for me long before this story ever began.

Finally, this acknowledgement is the first small installment in a long repayment plan to my wonderful husband Jose, without whose constant support and encouragement, none of this would have happened. You took your time showing up, but I'm so glad we found one another. Thank you for every day.

Lisa Manterfield is the creator of

LifeWithoutBaby.com, an online forum that gives a voice to women without children. Her writing has been featured in *Los Angeles Times, Bicycle Times,* and *Romantic Homes.* She lives with her husband and cat, and divides her time between Los Angeles and Santa Rosa, California.